PAGE 156 ?

# LAPSES IN SYNAPSES

# LAPSES IN SYNAPSES

## THE RANDOM LOGIC

## AND GENERAL CHAOS OF

## WHIT DESCHNER

The Eddie Tern Press

Atlantis, El Dorado, Camelot, Valhalla,
Freeloadia, Shangra La

☞ *A Horse Course* first appeared in *Horse and Rider* *Shutting the Door* and *I Didn't Say That* first appeared in *Inside Outside Magazine*

☞ The rest of the pieces first appeared out of nowhere then flashed across my screen before finally infecting my hard drive where they refused to come out unless put into book form.

☞ Cover and book design and much patience
   by Elizabeth Watson
☞ Edited by Sherry Nelson, Eloise Dielman,
   Marquita Green

☞ All pictures by Whit Deschner unless otherwise noted—which isn't very often

☞ Library of Congress Cataloging-in-Publication Date: Deschner Whit around 1953, 3:00 AM, Sunday
   1. Humor 2. Questionable Humor
3. Really Questionable Humor 4. Light Humor
5. Dark Humor 6.Questionable Dark Humor
7. Ridiculous Humor  8. Really Dark Questionable
Ridiculous Dodgy Humor 9. What's so Funny
Anyway? 10.Your Mudder Wears Army Boots
11. Size 12.

ISBN 978-0-9605388-1-2

Printed in the USA

THIS BOOK IS
DEDICATED TO MY WALLET

FOR SERIOUS DISEASE
MEET. DR. TRIPATHI
In Sri Ram Mandir...
ON ANY. TUESDAY

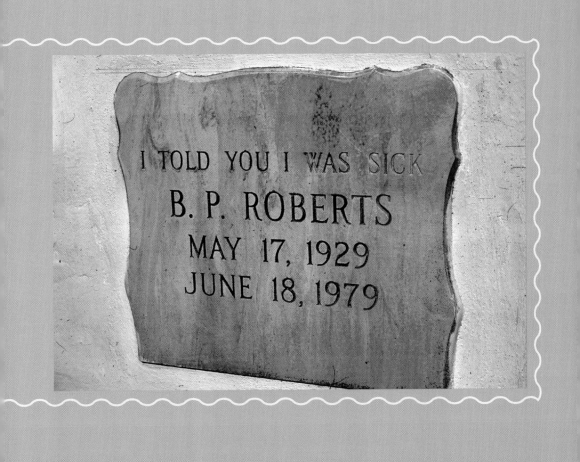

I TOLD YOU I WAS SICK
B. P. ROBERTS
MAY 17, 1929
JUNE 18, 1979

# CONTENTS

123

135

143

# A FOREWARNED FOREWORD

Of all the books I have sent to the galleys this one is unique. Manuscripts either come in neatly-wrapped mailed packages or they are sent electronically and always they are queried. This one came unannounced, unmarked and left on the doorstep in a brown paper bag. To call it a manuscript is using the term in its most liberal sense for it was mere notes scribbled on the back of old lottery tickets, unpaid bills and traffic violations. Scrawled on the bag was a name: Whit Deschner. Instead of trying to return it, Deschner's work went straight into Dempster our publishing house dumpster. Yet, the next morning, there it was once more abandoned at the front door. This process repeated itself over the next three days until finally I decided to burn it which I promptly set off to do. Then a tiny voice called out "Please don't burn me!" Or maybe I just imagined it. I hesitated. I wondered, "A manuscript with that much resolve must have something to say."

It didn't.

Yet after reading it there was **"PLEASE DON'T BURN ME!"**
something I liked about it. It intrigued me. It had that *je ne se qua*[1] feel. Despite the board of director's hostility towards the project I, single-handedly, went ahead in seeing this Whit Deschner person's manuscript was given a good home. This then is what was pieced together—what you are holding and perhaps contemplating burning yourself. His book. It is the book I can only hope and imagine this mystery person Whit Deschner had in mind. I have no way of knowing. How could I know? He never returned my phone calls.

Trying to find out about Deschner's life to write for this intro has been just that: trying. What little there is on the web about him is either wrong or contradictory. People I asked who admitted knowing him had at first genuine excitement in their voice. That is until they discovered I was not the carrier of the money they claimed he owed them. Nor could I pin down exactly where he lives; supposedly, eastern Oregon and yet other sources maintain he resides in the small Principality of Freeloadia— which I never knew existed but it indeed does. (Look close at a map and you'll see it sandwiched between the Diminutive Republic and the Philander Isles.) When I called the operator for Freeloadia's country code she thought I was joking then tried humoring me saying she didn't have it off hand and that she'd call me back. She never did.

What I did discover about Deschner is the tragedy of his life. He has suffered immensely from chronic procrastination. He even put off his birth mark until he was two years old. On the other hand I found in his notes his bragging about rarely getting writer's block. He rarely got it he maintained because he rarely wrote. My calls to his doctor to research Deschner's malady were not returned. Nor did his psychiatrists call me back.

Another strange tidbit concerning Deschner's life showed up in an anonymous envelope from one Richard Lemmy, Keswick's unofficial poet laureate.

---

[1] That's French

T-WIT-TO-WOO

T-WIT-TO-WHOM

The poem reads:

*Our Yankee friend this very night*
*Went for an evening prowl,*
*When from the woods above the path*
*Came the call of the lonesome owl.*
*'T-wit-to-woo' the birdie called, on his branch he stood erect.*
*'T-wit-to-whom' the Yankee said, 'is technically correct.'*
*'So who are you' the foul replied, 'to whom do I refer?'*
*'It is to Whit to who you speak, you curious old bird'*
*'Whit who? You twit!' the feathered friend of the Yankee then inquired*
*'Just Whit to you, I think you'll find is all that is required.'*
*Then called a bird, to wit the owl, to Whit the twit below*
*'Who is who and am I you? It does confuse me so.'*
*I was further down the track and first I was amused*
*But who was who and was Whit it—I quickly grew confused.*
*I intervened to save our friend, I clutched and pulled him free*
*So here he is our Yankee friend, fresh and off his tree.*

I wrote to Mr. Lemmy asking if his poem had some sort of meaning. He never replied to my letter.

And so not knowing much about the writer we have to judge his character by his writing, which perhaps leaves even more confusion about the person. Whether the humor in this book is funny or not depends (and, if not is it still humor?). It certainly is not dry but then again who ever heard of wet humor? Some is dark, a lot is light, but again; an again, who ever heard of heavy humor? Nor do we know what is real and unreal, fact or fiction. The one constant of this book is that the humor is not consistent as Deschner tries explaining in his forward. Not everyone is seen being amused by Deschner's sense of (or lack of) humor. His book, *Travels with a Kayak* won a national award for humor but supposedly, the lone dissenting judge saw to it he was not invited to the awards ceremony. My calls to the organization that award the awards to confirm this story were not returned.

So for better or for worse, good or bad here, against the board of directors' original recommendation to shred and burn the manuscript, I have gone ahead with the book's publication. So far Unemployment has not returned my calls.

Bill Harzia
Ex-Editor in Chief
The Eddie Tern Press

JUST WHIT TO YOU

# A BACKWARDS FOREWORD

**W**hile writing the foreword to this collection of stories, I asked myself, why is it that a foreword is the last thing written in a book? This should really be a backword because I have come to realize it's because only then the writer (me) tries understanding and explaining what they have written or thought they have written to convince you (the reader) that they knew what they were doing all along. This usually takes the shape of an apology or an excuse painted liberally with righteous justification. As a last resort they stick in pictures. Most times the writer (me) is clueless. An example:

Ten years ago I was diagnosed with Parkinson's, a cruel cosmic joke, but over time I began seeing humor with the disease. Hoping for a book to grow from it I began writing. It grew all right, much like a bonsai tree is nurtured. After ten years I hardly had enough material to make a large pamphlet. So I cheated and I stole. Thanks to slothfulness being the unwed mother to shortcuts, I stole other pieces I had written over the last 20 years, justifying that all the stories were humorous (at least to me anyway) despite the humor being different subspecies. Then I thought: readers (you again) becoming critics might grumble, "There's no consistency to this book."

"But," I answer, "There is: It is consistently inconsistent."

Besides, why should the alleged humor in this book be consistent when you (the reader) are hardly consistent in

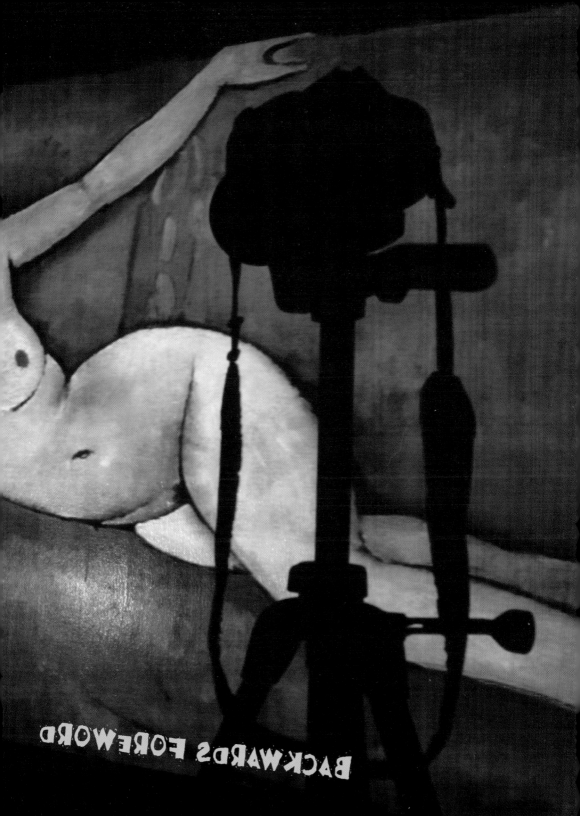

BACKWARDS FOREWORD

what you laugh at? The fact that some things aren't funny to some makes it all the funnier; like the time while cleaning red paint from a brush in my shop I suddenly I got the urge to splash HELTER-SKELTER on my girlfriend's cream colored cabinet. This, I also found out, was not funny. It was not even amusing.

Funny often and simply depends on what side of the fence you are on. Literally. Like the day I was in my yard when a small gang of motorcyclists raced down my driveway, skidded to a stop in a thunderhead of dust and yelled t me. "Hey man! Ya got a hose?"

"What do you need a hose for?"

"We're going to siphon gas from that truck."

"The hell you are!"

"No, we just talked to the owner and he says it's OK."

"Well I happen to be the owner and it's not OK."

"No, we just met him. Guy just down the road with the backhoe. Told us to take all the gas we wanted. Said to get it out of the truck."

Just then I saw my neighbor slowing driving by, laughing.

"There he goes, that's him!" one of them said.

Although amused, I failed to see the hilarity my neighbor saw in this just like he didn't see the humor that I saw when, after Christmas, he started getting calls about the ad in the paper offering top dollar for used Christmas trees. Soon, however, the tides turned again and he tickled himself pink when he placed an ad in the Nickel offering to give away all my horses, goats, basset hounds and pig and had me billed for it. This was certainly nothing to laugh at and I was forced to take inventory of all his stock and all his equipment so that I could put up posters around the county to auction off his ranch. I still smile at the shock on his face. But enough talk of horseplay.

For me humor has always been both my defense and defiance mechanism. When I was diagnosed with Parkinson's, I had to readjust my bar: lower or higher—perhaps sideways—I'm not sure which but it gave me a new perspective to write and to live from. Take the following incident in Bhutan: Had I not had Parkinson's (P.D.) I would have still been on a normal hike to a hot springs and back. I would have also gotten

HAD I NOT HAD PARKINSON'S
I WOULD HAVE STILL BEEN ON A NORMAL
HIKE TO A HOT SPRINGS AND BACK.

# ACTION AUCTION

## *Alan Smitty* Action Auctioneer 800 519 2088

**Moving auction for Mike and Terri Hutton** who have bought an Emu farm in Woy Woy Australia. Auction to be held at their ranch, 45794 Lower Bridge Rd. Go to milepost 21, turn Left on Lower Middle Bridge Rd, 3 miles on right. Auction will be well marked. Begins at 10:00 AM PST sharp  April 1st Mike will serve hamburgers Restrooms available. You will need them.

## TRACTORS

1991 John Deere 4755 Tractor, 4,335 Hours, 18.4R42 Rear Tires w/ Axle Mount Duals, Triple Hydraulics, Quick Hitch, 1000 lb. Inside Rear Wheel Weights, Otter 12 ft. Manual Angle Dozer, new gas cap

1969 John Deere 4020 Tractor, Synchro Range Transmission, 6,877 Hours, 18.4R34 Rear Tires, 4 Front Weights, replaced muffler

Case 1816B Uni Loader, 698 Hours, Onan 20 hp Engine, 44" Bucket, 15" Tires bald as Kojak

## EQUIPMENT

1996 John Deere 9500 Combine, 2,257 Engine Hours, 1,561 Separator Hours, 24.5-32 Front Tires, 14.9x24 Rear Tires, Chopper, Runs like crap John Deere 924 Platform Head

Speed King 52 ft., 8" Electric Drive Auger w/Farm Power Phase Converter, 15 hp  almost a 3 phase Motor

Ditch Witch J20 Trencher, Model 420, 2 cyl. Wisconsin Eng., 48" Bar,

## TRUCKS

1997 GMC 350 3/4 Ton Pickup, Power Windows, Power Locks, Cruise Control, Air 97,000 miles One Owner good mileage on down hill

16 ft. Tandem Axle Utility Trailer, Wood floor, Ramps, Beaver Tail, 15" Tires Beaver not included

John Deere 3 pt. 5 Bottom Plow

3 Section Drag Harrow

John Deere 24 ft. Spring Tooth, Manual Fold

Heston swather

John Deere F25 Mower, Front Deck, 48" Cut w/Bagger

John Deere Gas Powered Weed Eater

12 V RV Sprayer

Honda KD 125 Motorcycle

## MISCELLANEOUS

Vermeer 2 Bale 3 pt. Carrier

125 Gal. LP Tank

500 Gal. Fuel Tank, 12 V. Pump

Pickup Tool Boxes

Aluminum Ladders

Septic Tank Pump

Used septic tank includes contents

Hammer w/o handle

Entire collection of David Cassidy albums

And way too much other junk to mention here

## STOCK

2 Horses goose-rumped, herring-gut, cow-hocked in back pigeon-toed in front, mutton-wither, both blind in one eye, one left, one right, make excellent pair

18 registered Hereford bulls free range. Good luck catching them. 3 of them gay

35 - 2nd and 3rd year re-bred heifers

278 pairs various brands, many breeds, several buffalo

78 old cows toothless excellent gums

## RANCH

2,410  irrigated acres if it rains. Soil is composed of mostly metamorphic rock. Fences, where standing, in good condition. Barn, shop. 4 bedroom 2 bath older ranch house Needs no air conditioning if wind blows. House contains various but entire eco-systems.

lost because I took a shortcut—and it was a shortcut too but not the one I needed. This one came out just 300 feet above where I was going not to mention the river I somehow needed to cross. Since I wanted to arrive in live condition, I turned back. It began to rain. I ducked under the eaves of a local's yak shed to dig out my raincoat from my pack. I was hoping to go unnoticed but that was wishful thinking. A small boy found me, ran off to announce his find and before I could leave I was surrounded by every family within the five zip codes. Had I been normal nothing would have happened because nothing happens to normal people. But my left arm began to shake, something my new audience quickly noticed. Of course there was no common word between us except for OK and Coca Cola but it was easy enough to understand what was being said.

> ☞ Look the Westerner is shivering; he must be cold.
> ☜ But it is hot out.
> ☞ I know but they are different, only half of him is cold; he is only shaking on one side.
> ☜ Yeah, his west side, that's why he's called a westerner.
> (Much laughter)
> ☞ Uygen, tell your mother to make him some tea.
> Five minutes later Uygen's mother's tea was all gone.
> ☜ Look he still is shaking. Uygen! Fetch more tea!
> Again, same thing.
> ☞ Uygen, the Westerner needs more warming.
> Go fetch some firewood!

They built a small fire and motioned me next to it. Growing warm I began taking my raincoat off. They shook their heads and told me to stop. They insisted I drink more tea. Soon I feared they would be water-boarding me with it.

> ☞ Stupid westerner. We build him a fire to warm him and although he is still shivering, he starts taking off his clothes. Uygen fetch more wood, we'll get him warm yet.

They built the fire up and had they pushed me any closer I would have spontaneously combusted. I didn't wish to be rude to my hosts but an hour-and-a-half had passed and I needed to first find my trail so I could get off of it before dark. I left, but not before they commented,

> ☞ Strange lot those Westerners. Don't even know when it's cold or hot out.

Eventually I found my way and as I trotted off down the correct trail, I thought, "What a lucky guy I am. I have something funny to write."

So here it is. My book. I still haven't a clue how to introduce it. Nor am I exactly sure what it's about other than I hope it puts a smile on (you the reader) your face. The world is too serious not to laugh at. I mean, heck, I don't even take humor seriously… And if you can't read then I put in some pictures for you.

Otherwise you can write to:

Complaints room 48721
Building 276, Section 47a
89765 Avenue de la Bendrologie
District de la Zogona
Ouagagdougou
Burkina Faso

**IF YOU CAN'T READ THEN I PUT IN SOME PICTURES FOR YOU.**

All complaints must include a picture of yourself naked, an SASE paper-clipped to 100 Bulgarian Stotinkas. (Kwatchas will no longer be accepted.) All complaints must be 50 words or less and be written in Swahili. Complaints not meeting these requirements will be published. Please allow at least 15 years for a reply.

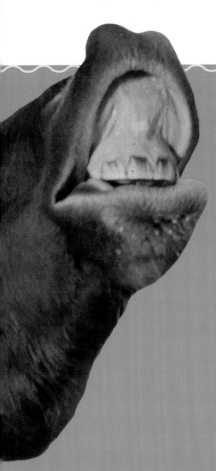

# MANe THAT TUNe

The lion's biggest problem

Lies within its snore.

Even while he is sleeping

He does so with a roar.

## THE VULTURE

The vulture won't hurt you

Patience is his virtue.

He'll just wait till you're dead

So he can be fed.

# GREEN ACRES:

# THE NEXT GENERA

# CHAPTER

# 1

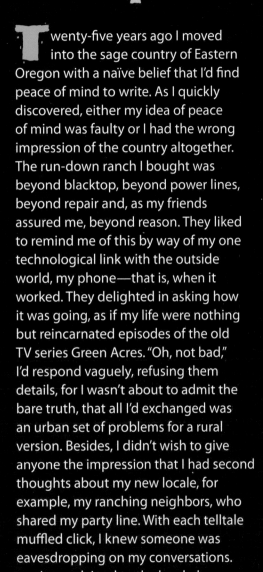

Twenty-five years ago I moved into the sage country of Eastern Oregon with a naïve belief that I'd find peace of mind to write. As I quickly discovered, either my idea of peace of mind was faulty or I had the wrong impression of the country altogether. The run-down ranch I bought was beyond blacktop, beyond power lines, beyond repair and, as my friends assured me, beyond reason. They liked to remind me of this by way of my one technological link with the outside world, my phone—that is, when it worked. They delighted in asking how it was going, as if my life were nothing but reincarnated episodes of the old TV series Green Acres. "Oh, not bad," I'd respond vaguely, refusing them details, for I wasn't about to admit the bare truth, that all I'd exchanged was an urban set of problems for a rural version. Besides, I didn't wish to give anyone the impression that I had second thoughts about my new locale, for example, my ranching neighbors, who shared my party line. With each telltale muffled click, I knew someone was eavesdropping on my conversations.

I complained to the local phone company, a family-run operation. I requested a private line. The secretary, Ma, ushered me in to see the president, Pa, a man who presided over two hundred and fifty numbers. He looked like he was more adept at connecting a milking machine to a cow than a phone to a jack. Distantly, I swore I could hear the theme song to Green Acres begin. I said, "I'd like a private line."

He responded by laughing, and then tucked a plug of tobacco into his lip. He waited for the tobacco to kick in, and then spoke, "You know what I call your line?"

I shook my head.

"A charity operation. Seventeen miles of cable to service just seven households. You're lucky to have a party line."

Soon after this conversation, in Green Acres fashion, the problem solved itself in its own twisted way. The intrusions started diminishing because my phone, a host to numerous petty natural disasters, began going dead with increasing frequency. Our seven-household charity line, running through the sage, was strung on what looked like the very poles that put the Pony Express out of business; bull pine accommodated it through a small forest. Where it broke out across the sage again, more skewed poles carried it to my land, where fence posts and a willow tree ushered it unceremoniously into the side of my house. Thanks to the activity of lightning strikes and windstorms and falling trees, days began passing without service. Not that I'm going to admit I really started missing it. Once I watched my phone, as if of its own possessed initiative, take a flying leap off its perch and accelerate across the floor only to slam into the wall before it lay still once more. Just then my wide-eyed gaze glimpsed my neighbor's bull trotting out the driveway, his legs ensnared in my phone line.

Another time, when my phone remained dead for three weeks, I prorated my bill for the missing segment, and was duly informed, via mail, that I first had to notify the phone company of the outage in order for my arithmetic to be honored.

"How," I later demanded of president Pa, "am I supposed to notify you that my phone is out, if my phone is out?"

"Reg'lations," Pa said, shrugging, trying not to lose the snoose out of his cupped lip.

I said, "Well, I'm still not paying for that portion."

"We'll cut off your phone," he threatened.

"How are you going to do that if it's already cut off?" I wanted to know.

The brief ensuing standoff dissolved when I towed his daughter's car out of the barrow pit. As if by magic my phone began working, and my bill was absolved of any outstanding balance.

Throughout all this, I was more determined than ever to write. My agent, confirming the doubts she was having about me, complained, "I can never reach you by phone.

What if I need to get a hold of you quickly?"

"You can write me."

"But that's three or four days."

"You wouldn't believe how quick that's considered around here."

"Can't you get a fax machine?"

"No," I answered, "Because my phone line won't carry it. Don't you hear that static?"

"Static?"

"Well, some of it is gunshots."

"You mean you have people with guns there?"

"All the time. Can't be much different than New York."

"But what do they shoot?"

"Varies—ground squirrels, starlings, road signs. Why, just three months ago my neighbor shot his wife."

"You're kidding! What did he get?"

"Another one. It's hard to keep wives around here. There's bears and no shopping. Heck we can't even get a washing machine to work up here."

"Why's that?"

"No electricity."

"It's off?"

"Nope, don't have it."

> HOW AM I SUPPOSED TO NOTIFY YOU THAT MY PHONE IS OUT, IF MY PHONE IS OUT?

"You don't have electricity!" she repeated incredulously, then trying to regain her nerve, posed her next question slowly. "But if . . . you . . . um, don't have . . . electricity, how . . . um, can you write?"

"Typewriter," I said, and with the silence that followed, I thought she'd fainted.

Years passed and perhaps my quandaries would have remained at the old Green Acres pace of life if technology hadn't changed the script. Even my friends incessantly asked, "How can you write without a word processor?" I didn't like the way their question teased the fact that my typewriter kept breaking down. I could revert to pen and paper, but my writing would have to be transcribed. So at last I knuckled under. Not only did I buy a computer, having to learn its suspect language, I bought a generator to feed it electricity. Suddenly I was assassinating the quiet I'd sought in the country. Besides, my generator was an ill-tempered beast, and it enjoyed vindictively strangling my electricity at will. Watching my screen shrivel and die became a common occurrence; I started spending more time looking for lost files

than writing them. I wondered how Eddie Albert would have coped? Then I thought, "Heck! Eddie would have spent at least three shows installing solar panels!"

My solar system returned me once more to the tranquility of the country—just the gentle whir of my computer fan, punctuated by the occasional road sign being shot. On sunny days I could write to my heart's content, but when clouds or night bruised the sky I had to ration my adjectives. And just when I concluded I could live forever amidst the happy marriage of ultramodern technology and country living, two home wreckers appeared on the figurative horizon.

One, the Rural Electrification Act, blew my local ma and pa phone company a million-dollar windfall to replace our charity line with fiber optic cable—whether we wanted it or not. And the second item? That damn fool who invented the Internet.

I tried ignoring what implications these threatening advances in technology might mean, along with parrying friends' new nagging question, "When are you going to get e-mail?" Before I could answer, they launched into exalting the virtues of the Internet. I still believe I could have withstood this new round of peer pressure if one of my friends hadn't accused me of being a visionary. He said, "Years ago I thought you were nuts, moving to the country, but now I think all you've got to do is log onto the Internet and you've got it made."

Not that I ever wanted to be a visionary; I just reckoned this was a cheap opportunity to become one and see what it felt like. I bought a new computer and a modem. But, once again, if I thought fate was going to conspire with me, I was mistaken. I'll admit I was genuinely excited when I loaded my new online program into my computer. I turned it on and marveled how quietly my computer dialed its service number, so quietly that I didn't even hear it. Then, nothing happened.

I picked up my phone. Dead. My neighbor had discovered the phone line with his back hoe. After what seemed like several nuclear winters for the line to be patched—lightning struck a relay box; and when that break was spliced back together, fiber-optic deficient gophers began attacking the cable. Even when the line was supposedly fixed and I could talk on the phone, the connection refused to accommodate my online service. Not once could I log on.

Fuming, I drove down to protest to the snoose-chewing phone company owner once more. Gazing at me as if I had three heads, he said, "Weren't you the one who always complained about being on a party line?"

"I was," I replied, not knowing where he was herding his fuzzy logic.

His sudden laugh should have given me a clue. "And now you can't get on the Internet? Why, don't cha know? That's the biggest party line on earth!"

Since then, I've given up on the Internet. And I still think about Green Acres. In fact I'm going to write an updated version. I'm going to call it *Green Acres: The Next Generation*. A Rod Sterling sound-alike will introduce it.

# DEADER N' A DOORNAIL

REALTOR

REALITY

**W**alking into local realty offices, we'd announce, "We're looking for a place in the country." In retrospect I suppose my partner, Carol, and I were a flawless portrait of naïveté. As we described our ideal place we quickly came to learn what hands rubbing together under desks sounded like. We desired an old small farmhouse insulated by acres of land. We wanted a view. We wanted a stream or maybe a pond. We wanted a tranquility that was disturbed by nothing more than bird tunes and coyote voice-mailing each other. Sooner than later, the realtors would interrupt and ask, "And what price range are we looking at?"

We also learned what the immediate silence of hands that stop rubbing together under desks sounded like. This was inevitably followed by one of two facial expressions. The first was an inadequately-concealed wince leading to a polite but immediate jettison from that particular realtor's universe. The second look was one of stoic resolve. Even as neophytes it was easy for us to read. It said, "If I can sell you a place I'll clinch the salesman hero-of-the-year trophy."

Needless to say, what intimacy we developed with realtors came with this second batch. They were a colorful bunch and all took their turn swinging wildly at our fixed notion like blindfolded maniacs attacking a piñata. Although their approaches varied, they did hold one thing in common—our hunted "place in the country" meant that any listing outside town limits was fair game. Four realtors in particular enlightened our concept of the industry: Colonel Parker, Tex, Millhouse and Mrs. Unitas—not their real names, of course.

Tex was a pseudo cowboy who dressed in the whole nine-yard garb—a ridiculous hat, a belt buckle as big as a deformed hubcap, the telltale wear mark and bulge of a snoose can in his back jeans pocket, and snakeskin cowboy boots. Between lipfuls of snoose, he detailed the features of his "sweethearts"—his good –ol' boy name for his listings. Tex's world, as we quickly discovered, was highly imaginative. His "sweethearts" were anything but, and their features pure fantasy. As for Tex if he had to match his cowboy wits against a cow, we were certain he would be hopelessly outmaneuvered. Not so slowly, cracks in Tex's facade began to show: he didn't want to scratch his pickup, rattlesnakes caused him no end of panic and, the clincher, one day he spent at least ten minutes cleaning cow effluence off one of his boots as the result of a misplaced step. After that day, Tex quickly faded from our lives like an old battery. Maybe, deep down, he knew we would never have bought one of his "sweethearts" anyway; shallower though, I think he suspected that we saw him for what he wasn't.

Overfilling Tex's void came, Millhouse, the wannabe politician. To this day, Carol and I each accuse each other of soliciting his help. In any case, one day he was simply upon us like bad weather, only bad weather doesn't smell like cheap cologne. Millhouse also wore a fixed grin and a toupee that hung on his head like a lenticular cloud and with these two items firmly in place, he set to work on us, employing every cheap sales trick known in sleazedom. While locking in eye contact he pumped my hand until my wrist grew hot with tendonitis. Carol, who he turned to next, wisely kept her hand to herself, quickly parrying away his eye gimmick with a glare I'd only seen her employ on stray dogs. Actually we dealt with Millhouse only for half a day but when it was over it felt like half a millennium. The first listing he showed us was one that Tex had already tried to shoehorn us into, but Millhouse dressed it up in an entirely new set of distorted semantics. The other place was an old abandoned homestead, a skeleton of a house sitting in the middle of a quarter section of scab rock. I'll admit the place had a country feel to it but I think it was the trespassing cows wandering through the house that gave me this impression. A tiny creek ran not by but underneath the house. I said, "You didn't tell us that a river ran through it."

But Millhouse didn't understand subtle sarcasm. Instead he replied, "That's the sweetest water you'll ever taste."

"Even if we chase the cows out?" Carol asked.

It took us several hours to convince Millhouse we were definitely not interested and that it would be far easier to refurbish the Sistine chapel than to reconstruct the wreckage before our eyes.

MILLHOUSE ALSO WORE A FIXED GRIN AND A TOUPEE THAT HUNG ON HIS HEAD LIKE A LENTICULAR CLOUD.

# I ASKED HIM WHAT HE THOUGHT THE R-VALUE OF THE STARLING NESTS IN THE WALLS MIGHT BE.

I asked him what he thought the R-value of the starling nests in the walls might be and he finally shut up—for a while. Driving back to town, Millhouse acted plenty sour, yet it was in his genes to sell us something, anything; and soon, as his face uncurdled, he began selling us himself. He was running for state legislature he informed us. He really didn't want to run, but selfish agricultural zoning laws were keeping him from quick millions. Dropping us off, he said he'd call on us tomorrow. The next time we saw his face was several months later. His picture was on the front page of the town's paper with a headline that read, "Local Realtor Wins Seat."

Next we solicited Colonel Parker's help—another mistake. The Colonel was in his mid-sixties and his clothes fit him like cotton sacks stuffed haphazardly past capacity. He wore a hearing aid in his left ear and an unlit cigar stub in his mouth. As we immediately discovered, the Colonel's lone tactic was simple: he would not take "no" for an answer simply because his hearing aid only worked at his convenience.

His listings he called "undiscovered gems" but, like everything else we had seen, the Colonel's "gems" were, at best, rhinestones in the rough no matter how he lavished them. Showing us his undiscovered gems, he would strategically plant himself between Carol and me; once he even managed to wrap his arms around both our shoulders. I'll have to admit it was an effective method for keeping Carol and me from rolling our eyes at one another.

I wish I could have called the Colonel "endearing" but he was far from it, nor were we sure how to rid ourselves of him; fortunately, it happened by accident. On the side we began seeing Mrs. Unitas and the Colonel caught wind of it. Fortunately, his character make-up included being a chauvinist hog. Had we been seeing a rival male realtor I think Colonel Parker might have grudgingly swallowed the fact, but a woman doing his job was outright sacrilege. He was so disgusted that later, when we accidentally ran into him, he refused to even acknowledge us.

Yet from the Colonel to Mrs. Unitas was a leap from a frying pan into a very hot fire. Mrs. Unitas was the most aggressive person I've ever met in my life. Her husband was a freshly-retired pro football player and, as she often implied, if we bought from her there would real prestige involved. Yep, we could actually brag how we'd bought from the wife of some chump who currently had no tangible work skills in the county except to buck hay. Although Mrs. Unitas also carried a bag of cheap tricks, her primary battle plan was one of simple extortion: either we bought a place from her or she promised to become a permanent fixture in our deedless lives.

# IT APPEARED OUR NUMBER HAD BEOME THE NUMERICAL SYNONYM OF DEJECTION

"You're going to just love this one," she would assure us each time we set out to go look at yet another listing. And upon arrival at the prospect she would lean close to us and, in a conspirative whisper, as if someone was hiding in the sagebrush that might overhear the deal we were about to be let in on, she would say, "This is just the place you want!"

However, most of the places that we supposedly wanted would have required that we evict an entire ecosystem in order to move into them.

Once, looking at yet another place that was more breeze than substance and looked as though it had been the recipient of an infinite number of natural disasters, Mrs. Unitas exclaimed, brimming with fraudulent excitement, "Now this is exactly the place you want. You're looking at country living at its best."

"I'd hate to see it at its worst," Carol whispered.

Carol and I just stood there in stunned silence. She mistook our quiet as contemplation.

"This is a very good buy," she assured us. "Tomorrow might be too late."

"We'll take our chances," Carol informed her.

"I was keeping your budget in mind," she said sharply. "Realistically, you are going to have to move your goalpost a little closer to what you can afford."

I thought, "Moving a goalpost—I bet her husband taught her that one."

"Look," she continued as the irritation in her voice grew, "I know what you've been looking for. You can't have everything and this is it!"

I threw up my hands; I'd had enough. "You're insulting us showing us this trash."

I wanted to say more but she cut me off. "Listen," she said in an even tone through teeth that were almost clinched, "If you want a place with everything, we can go look at one. But I guarantee you, even with creative financing, you won't touch it."

On the ride back to town Carol and I both rode in the back seat of Mrs. Unitas' car in silence. It felt like we'd been arrested. Booked on stubbornness.

After our fling with Mrs. Unitas our phone stopped ringing altogether and it appeared our number had become the numerical synonym of dejection; this was fine with us. Yet still, out of habit, we looked at the newspapers and sniffed the bait. Realty's great trade euphemisms were suddenly a snap for us to decipher. For example:

**BREATHTAKING VIEW** (Prevailing winds rarely will drop below 60 m.p.h. making it hard to breathe.)

**HANDYMAN'S DELIGHT** (If you ever finish patching this house to a point suitable for human habitation you could get a doctorate in carpentry. If not, you'll at least be valedictorian in the nuthouse.)

**A RIVER RUNS THROUGH IT** ( . . . and will continue to do so with each spring runoff)

**SOUNDS OF SILENCE** (owned by a stone deaf person)

**SECLUDED GETAWAY** (which is what the last owner, a bank robber, was doing)

**SUPER LOCATION** (exactly halfway between the liquor store and the 7-11)

**UNIQUE LOG HOME** (thanks to what the carpenter ants have left)

**OWNER MOTIVATED TO SELL** (owner needs quick cash before litigation catches up with him)

**INVESTMENT PROPERTY** (Property is a great investment if Disneyland builds a cattle grazing theme park near it.)

**NOT MANY OF THESE LEFT** (Yes, but none of them are right either.)

During and after falling out with the town's realtors we had pursued private listings as well. But these fell neatly into two categories. The first were so far overpriced that even a realtor would have laughed at them. The second, the good deals, were snatched up quickly, or at least before we arrived.

So, just when we figured we'd been consigned to a permanent life of renting and those signatures on the Middle East Peace Accord would materialize long before our names ever became scrawled on any deed, our lucky strike struck. Out driving one day we passed by an old place with a sign that didn't say "For Sale" but "Garage Sale." We stopped in. Now there's a threadbare line about asking, "How much do you want for your garage?" I didn't use it, but we did end up buying the garage, along with the small old farmhouse, the stream, the pond, and the total tranquility that surrounded the place. It was an old retired couple who, due to their place's remoteness hadn't had much luck with their garage sale. As we talked they explained how they were getting ready to sell the place. As for their price? We bought it for exactly what I told the realtors we had to spend. Occasionally we get letters from the old couple. They live in Mexico now and tell us how they always wanted a place on the beach.

سید مقبول شاہ دندانس

D MAQBOOL SHAH DENTIST

# CHAPTER

# 3

If women did originate on Venus there were horses there, too, and lush habitat where both species peacefully cohabited. This is why women unconditionally, uncontrollably, irresponsibly and irrationally love horses. Mars, the red planet, had no grass thus no horses, which is exactly why, if I had chosen to live by myself, I would have had no horses.

Thanks to my sister, my horse history began at a young age. By the age of seven she'd gone pigeon-toed and bowlegged just from reading Black Beauty and seeing National Velvet. Instantly, she became one of the world's leading authorities on horses. Coincidentally, around that time my parents naïvely decided to vacation in the Rockies. As we passed each horseback riding outfit (approximately one every half mile or so) my sister demanded that we stop, and my parents, poor terrorist negotiators that they were, all too often did so. As consolation, being younger and smaller, I was always given to the cowboy named "Red" or "Butch" or Corky" who put me on the blind pony that wandered off the trail, the lame one that refused to move, or the gentle one that got stung by a hornet proving I had no future in bronc riding. It always ended in tears. I could have died of dehydration.

# "I WANT A HORSE, I WANT A HORSE, I WANT A HORSE."

For my sister, these rides were both bliss and an addiction. Naturally, she wanted her own horse and coming home she only repeated four words, "I want a horse, I want a horse, I want a horse." Our house was like a lunatic monastery with her moping around chanting her mantra. Psychiatric care would have been cheaper but instead my parents bought her Tonto.

To buy Tonto, my dad brought in a consultant: Howard, our neighbor. Howard's sole horse expertise lay in the fact that he was from Montana. He reiterated this fact by wearing a cowboy hat when he mowed his lawn only he referred to it as "hayin'." Forty-five years later, I can tell you that I have yet to meet a real cowboy named Howard. None would keep such a name. Howard couldn't tell the difference between a gaskin and a gas can, but he declared Tonto a fine animal and Tonto was ours.

I'm not sure if Tonto was a paint or a pinto, and I still don't know the difference. I do know he had a brown tail and that he was part carnivore; I still carry the teeth marks on my shoulder. I also know that the span of time my sister owned Tonto was

like a geologic time period in my family's history. Our lives centered entirely around him. Sleep, meals, all times of day were interrupted by shouts of, "He's out!" "He's in the garden!" "He's in the neighbor's garden!" "He's heading down the road!"

Heading down the road Tonto did under his own initiative, never with a rider. If it wasn't his idea, he wasn't about to move. If Tonto had been Paul Revere's horse we'd still be under British rule. And, if my parents had been smarter they would have snuck out in the night, haltered him and threatened to lead him. He would have stood there frozen, legs locked, and with his emergency brake on and they could have plastered him and sold him as a statue.

# "HE'S OUT!" "HE'S IN THE NEIGHBOR'S GARDEN!" "HE'S HEADING DOWN THE ROAD!"

Tonto's other specialty was fence demolition. Other pastures weren't greener, it was just that my mom's garden was outside his fence. To solve this problem Tonto would strategically place his butt on the fence, engage in reverse and not quit until he was munching fresh pea vines. The Berlin wall would have fallen much sooner had Tonto been parked under it. As a result of his escaping, dad boarded out Tonto while he constructed a real fence, one with pole rails and railroad ties. When Tonto returned home three months later, he appeared completely reformed. During his sabbatical his tail had turned white and he had learned manners; he was so polite he even let my sister ride him. Walk, trot, canter, you name it, Tonto, as Howard had claimed, was a good horse.

Then the call came. The swearing was so loud I could hear it over the phone. Dad had picked up the wrong horse. After a tense exchange the real Tonto was returned, and if the brown tail didn't reveal his old self his fence demolition did. Within the hour Tonto had backed through dad's new fence. And my sister, thinking Tonto might actually be reformed hopped on his back and was promptly launched into orbit. Her arm broke her fall. Her fall broke her arm. It wasn't long after that Tonto mysteriously disappeared.

For twenty-five years my life remained horseless. And if some fortune-teller would have predicted that I was about to own a ranch with too many horses to count, I would have had them arrested for malpractice. The horses were not my idea. They were my partner's. Carol had her intentions, ones I learned of when a small brown package arrived, addressed to her. Inside was a black leather bridle. She held it up with admiration. "It was my mother's," she exclaimed.

"I didn't know she wore one," I answered.

Several hours passed before our relationship settled down once more onto speaking terms. At last I asked, "What's the bridle for?"

Although I've never really thought how people gawked at Rip Van Winkle returning from his sleep, I now knew from the look Carol supplied me. "A horse," she said incredulously.

After this, the horse magazines came out into the open. Carol perused them the way I used to study Sears Christmas catalogs as a kid. And in her enthusiasm she began to imagine that I was just as excited about horses as she was, and she would show me picture after picture of horses.

"Oh! Just look at this one!" she would exclaim.

"You showed me that one already."

"No, I didn't. I showed you this one."

"That's just another picture of him."

"No it's not. Oh! Look here! It's a miniature. Isn't he darling?"

"I suppose. Why don't you buy one."

"I just said he was darling, I didn't say I wanted one. I want a horse I can ride."

"Sure, but think of the advantages of a miniature horse. I don't have to build a

barn; we can buy a doghouse for him instead and muck it out with a trowel. It'd save the expense of buying a pitchfork."

Around this time, I began hearing a new perversion of English, something I call the shared personal pronoun: *my* became *ours* and *I* became *we*, as in, "*Our* truck is big enough to pull a horse trailer isn't it?"

"What horse trailer?"

"The one *we* are going to buy."

Looking at trailers I realized the situation had gone past the point of no return and I lamented that Carol's interest wasn't for a cheaper sport like say flying or yachting or just a good sound heroin addiction. Soon after the arrival of the horse trailer Carol said she had at last decided on a horse to buy. "I've decided on a quarter horse," she declared.

"And what kind of animal are the other three-fourths?"

"Don't be funny. It comes with papers."

"You mean it's not house-trained?"

The horse looked innocent enough but so do baby rattlesnakes. Carol said his name was Western Regal, a name she insisted I use, until Delbert, the neighbor, showed up. He looked at the horse once in what appeared disbelief, and then he looked even more intensely as if the horse was translucent and he was trying to see right through it. Delbert circumnavigated it several times, studied it even harder, took off his hat, scratched his head, scratched his whiskers and said, "Yep, same snip on the nose, same herring-gut,

> I BEGAN HEARING A NEW PERVERSION OF ENGLISH, SOMETHING I CALL THE SHARED PERSONAL PRONOUN: MY BECAME OURS AND I BECAME WE, AS IN, "OUR TRUCK IS BIG ENOUGH TO PULL A HORSE TRAILER ISN'T IT?"

same goose rump, pigeon-toed like hell in the front, cow-hocked in the back. Yep, that's the mutton-withered son-of-a-bitch alright—Old Killer."

"Killer?" I said concerned.

"His name."

"Why Killer?" Carol asked.

The rancher looked at her with a raised eyebrow, "Killed a hand over in the Tailor country."

The neighbor, noticing Carol's apprehension, said, "I wouldn't worry about it, he's so old now you'll be lucky if you can get him to move."

But Killer did move. Just the promise of food would incite him into a one-horse stampede. And there was nothing wrong with Killer's appetite. He would suck in several lungfuls of air, then his head would disappear into the manger and it wouldn't come out until every molecule of hay dust was gone.

Over the next six months, Carol rode Killer. She rode him for hours, making up for the lost and unhappy time when she didn't have a horse. And when she wasn't riding she groomed him as if he was going to some country club horse event. Killer, she said, was a good horse.

So I was confused when the second horse, Flash, a pregnant thoroughbred, showed up. You'd have thought it was the second coming of Pegasus.

"I thought you said Killer was a good horse."

"I did. But he needs company. I'm giving Killer to you."

I thought, "What the heck; learn to ride, see the country by horseback," but my ideas about this and Killer's differed. My thoughts were of good ole horse/man bonding, like Lee Marvin in *Cat Balou*—get on my horse, go for a long walk, and contemplate life. Killer's idea of letting me see the country was a Sputnik-type launch. The old up-into-the-stratosphere where by simple geometry, the higher you go the farther you see. At the apex of my projection I saw things clearly and in that epifocal moment I realized—Venus had soft grass to land on; Mars had rocks. Killer was back at the barn I was building before I hit the ground. Cow droppings cushioned my head, saving Killer from further darkening his reputation.

Carol commented that she'd never seen a ride quite like it.

"Next time," I said, "I'll save myself the trouble of saddling him up. I'll just go climb a tree, enjoy the view then jump out head first."

"Don't be bitter. You'll learn."

"If I live. The more I learn, the less I want to know."

"If you loved your horse he wouldn't have thrown you."

But Carol kept on expanding my knowledge. She tried explaining the different kinds of horses to me, that each breed is bred for its own unique purpose.

"They all look alike to me," I said.

"You can't tell the difference between Killer and Flash?"

"That each one has its own special way of sucking hay out of the manger like an industrial vacuum?"

"Go on!" she said, "You don't see the difference?"

"Well, yes, as a matter of fact, the quarter horse runs right over me to get to its food; the thoroughbred bites me."

When I at last understood the difference between a thoroughbred and a quarter horse, I actually felt good about myself. Insatiably, I learned more until I could, with pride, impart to an inferior non-horse person my vast knowledge: how to discern the tell-tale symptoms of a bad case of snaffles; that the best bit for a horse is undoubtedly the crupper; that it's best if a horse's gaskins are always full; how to avoid latego aboard a tall horse; and, above all else, that bridle paths should always be cut at least eight feet wide to let two horses safely pass in opposite directions. I was eager to know more. But the next installment of my education exploded my balloon.

"Now then, take my thoroughbred, for example," Carol began.

"OK."

"Well, it's not a thoroughbred."

"No? You said it was."

"It's a quarter horse."

"Then why do you always call it a thoroughbred?"

"Well, it is, but it's registered as a quarter horse."

"You mean there's fraud involved in this?"

"Absolutely not! You can still have more thoroughbred in a quarter horse and still call it a quarter horse."

"Has this gone to the Supreme Court?"

"Don't be ridiculous. Besides it depends on the registry."

"Who's running this registry anyway?"

"They're separate registries."

"You mean there's more than one of these racketeering schemes?"

"They are very organized."

"Yes," I thought, "so is the Mafia." But for diplomacy's sake I let it slide.

> WOMEN, FROM THE MOMENT OF CONCEPTION, DESIRE HORSES. FOR MEN IT IS, AT BEST, AN ACQUIRED TASTE, LIKE LEARNING TO ENJOY MONGOLIAN FIRE OIL.

I walked away, dismayed, defeated. And, you know? Here, as I sit writing, I look out the window. Carol is riding Flash. She is cantering in a large circle and appears perfectly content. Seems to me that when the geneticists follow our DNA maps to their last dead end, the ultimate difference, the distinguishing characteristic between men and women will be that women, from the moment of conception, desire horses. For men it is, at best, an acquired taste, like learning to enjoy Mongolian fire oil.

WOLVES

As you enter Idaho there's a sign that reads, "Idaho is too great to litter." But what it should read is, "Idaho is too illiterate to be great." What the state needs around it is a fence. Forget Mexico. Without a fence, they are moving in: white supremacists, drivers who don't understand speed limits, senators with airport bathroom fetishes, and now wolves. It is what you'd expect from Idaho—and, it is being sanctioned. The wolf population is getting a recap because, Fish and Wildlife informs us, wolves are helping balance nature. But the pack that moved to my neighborhood were not signed on to any such accord and in my neighbor's lambing pen they offed nineteen of his lambs. Naturally this made local headlines and the following day the usual vocal minorities wrote their usual polarized letters to the editor. Perched on my fence I read the letters and realized I don't differ from any other hypocrite: To see a wolf running any direction but mine in wilderness beats Animal Planet hands down but then I wonder, wandering out to the woodshed in the middle of the night, will they be lurking in the dark, just waiting for me?

Thanks to the wolves' official spokesperson, this scenario is, fortunately, bogus. Such concerns over the last few years, with the reintroduction of the species, a special man/wolf bond has evolved: the radio collar. If I'm attacked by a wolf it's my own damn fault. In my neighbor's case one of the wolves was trapped, collared and re-released and—assuming wolves still run in packs— Fish & Wildlife can now follow the wolves and warn the rancher that the wolves are coming to eat nineteen of his sheep. So if I get et up by a wolf, I simply did not pay heed to the helicopters and planes and fleet of white pickups following the signal back and forth over my house and up and down the road. The constant added drone in the countryside is reassuring—more so than the U.N.'s black helicopters that I'm told trained here nightly to intimidate and wrest the world away from the Republicans and practice voodoo on the cattle. Planes, radio signals and wolves, it's all part of balancing nature, something I must get used to.

# WITHOUT SUCH EVIL THERE IS NO GOOD, SO MAYBE THERE IS SUCH A THING AS BALANCE.

So I think of the wolf throughout history, myth and literature; he/she/it's had mostly a bad rap. Without such evil there is no good so maybe there is such a thing as balance. I try to think of a good wolf and up pops the bitch that adopted and nursed Romulus and Remus before Social Services took them away and assigned them to humanoid parents. Still I bet the new parents couldn't break them of scratching fleas, sniffing crotches, butt scooting on the rugs and other repulsive traits not to mention Romulus' quick temper. Who is responsible for molding the twins' personalities is debatable but as far as Wikipedia knows Romulus did bump off Remus. It's spilt milk now; all parties involved are dead. It's a good thing it wasn't Remus who was on the fight as, "All roads lead to Reme," "Reme wasn't built in a day," and, "When in Reme do like the Remans" just doesn't cut it. Rome, at one time, might have been a good thing but just go and try and get a decent pizza there now. It wasn't the bitch's fault.

Think of all the negative connotations the poor wolf has had from college mascots to Nazi submarines and even Virginia Woolf. On the positive ledger, however, *Never Cry Wolf,* was a great read. Mostly though I think of fairy tales and perhaps it is here where our sub-conscious prejudice against wolves originates. Today, with the radio collars, technology and political correctness, these fairy tales can now be rewritten. Here's the Cliff Notes:

## THE BOY WHO CRIED WOLF

The collars alert the boy (previously an unemployable narcoleptic) that the wolves are stalking his flock; he calls no false alarms becoming so successful that he takes an

insomniac for a wife and he retires. Unfortunately his 401K goes south but with his AK–47 still working, he returns to herding.

## THE THREE LITTLE PIGS

Big Bad is a Muslim fanatic who blows things up instead of down. Fortunately with radio collars such terrorism is avoided; however, Hormel Factories go on triple red security alert anyway.

## LITTLE RED RIDING HOOD

Pretentiously skipping through the forest to Granma's with her peanut butter cookies, Red is nearly mowed down by a white Fish and Wildlife truck that is monitoring the wolf. The wolf is hightailing it to Granma's so he can welcome Red at the Granma's door. But Granma has gone to Walmart and instead the Wolf is greeted by a registered pedophile who has slipped his radio collar and is now cross-dressed in granny's clothes, waiting for Red. (He would've been there sooner but he had slowed down at the children's crossing.) Answering the knock on the door he opens it and

instead meets the wolf. "Ma-ma-ma-my, what a BIG radio collar you have on," stutters the pedophile just as Fish and Wildlife agents break down the back door. Granma returns stupidly happy from Walmart, happy to see the big bad sex offender arrested and hauled off and happy to see Red with her peanut butter cookies who got there late anyway. This all would be a warm and fuzzy happy ending except everyone dies of salmonella because they ate the peanut butter cookies.

Now regard "the balance of nature." Isn't this an oxymoron? The butcher has either one to ten digits on the scale. Now if we could get rid of half the world's population we might be able to release a few of those digits. On a trial basis we could at least start with Barry Manilow or Julio Iglesias. Proponents of the wolf reintroduction claim that wolves are an important link in the food chain. They take care of the overpopulations of deer and elk—along with my neighbor's sheep. And reducing the deer and elk populations restores watersheds, as studies have proved in Yellowstone. The deer and elk hang out in the riparian zone browsing away on the very stuff the beaver are trying to build dams and houses out of. Why the wolves don't huff and puff and eat the beaver instead is anyone's guess. With the success of the restored watershed, water bottling companies are bound to move in and, with a water bottling plant there we soon will see, *Old Faithful, Nature's Balance* plastic water bottles alongside every major highway.

# SO IS IT REALLY, TRULY NECESSARY TO BALANCE NATURE WITH AN ENTIRE SQUADRON OF HELICOPTERS AND PLANES?

So is it really truly necessary to balance nature with an entire squadron of helicopters and planes and traffic the roads with white—or any color pickups? With that much money to burn why don't we really burn it and smoke the wolves in the direction we want them to go. And if anyone really wishes to clean up watersheds why start in Yellowstone? Why don't we start on the Potomac; release some wolves there to reduce our own population. Do we really need all those senators and representatives?

In my education of wolf reintroduction I never realized wolves have their own spokesperson. This person fascinates me. It can't be easy being a wolf spokesperson especially when the wolves don't follow your script, like x-ing 19 lambs. Despite the fact we could do the same deed much quicker with a hand grenade, killing sheep as indiscriminately as these wolves did, infringes on our superiority as humans. The spokesperson most likely has a doctorate in denial. He bases his entire career focusing on less than ten words like: *supposedly, allegedly* and, *suspected;* then he paints every scenario possible except for connecting the obvious dots to a 19 lamb massacre. This is a man who—no matter what—does not cry wolf. He even has trouble saying the word. From the local newspaper:

"Due to the large size of the paw tracks and other factors the tracks are not coyote and that the tracks are bigger than coyote tracks. I am sure they are not coyote tracks . . . cougars have also been ruled out due to the shape of the prints, which is canine rather than feline, and the nature of the wounds to the lambs." (Thanks, I didn't know that.)

"In recent months we have found some wolf tracks five or six miles from here, near the forest line, but we have to trap or photograph the predator attacking the sheep to positively confirm that the attacks were the work of a wolf or wolves. I haven't ruled it out. There is that possibility. I am here to help solve the mystery of what killed their sheep." (Nice work, Watson.)

"Our role is to look at all the evidence and sort this out." (Very good, Watson.)

"The first thing we try to do is figure out what we are dealing with." (A confused public?)

"We haven't ruled wolves out in this situation. In a lot of cases we are able to rule wolves out. In this case we haven't ruled wolves out." (Watson, you're starting to annoy me.)

"Fish and Wildlife has investigated 42 reported wolf sightings but has not confirmed any of them. It is continuing to investigate as many as it can." (Batting average: Zero for 42. Who's your talent scout?)

"We take all the sightings seriously." (You must be joking!)

"We suspect they are here but are not 100 percent certain." (And 2 plus 2 is?)

"Investigating reports is difficult because wolves are secretive and move great distances. A wolf might travel 100 miles in a day." (Meaning you can't travel 100 miles a day to investigate?)

When a motorist spotted a wolf crossing the freeway and called Fish and Wildlife he was told there were no wolves in the region but was informed that wolf hybrids had been raised in that area in the past and there is a possibility that this was such an animal.

This guy should be a President spokesperson.

Imagine 20 years from now when some agency gets the brilliant idea to clone mastodons and reintroduce them into the wilderness. Imagine the quotes:

"Fish and Wildlife spokesperson Joe Maloney said, 'The tracks are bigger than elephant tracks. I'm sure they're not elephant tracks. Mainly because there are no elephants around here but you never know what escapes from the circus these days. Woolly mammoths have also been ruled out because we have not cloned one yet; however, that is not to say some other agency or country has cloned one and it has reintroduced itself into the area. Despite Mr. Brown's alleged spotting of a mastodon eating half his haystack and sexually molesting his harvester we do have to take into account that Mr. Brown does not see well when he drinks.'

# HE WOULD BE COMPENSATED—IF IT WERE PROVED IT WAS A MASTODON

"Brown claims his intoxication was induced after he saw the mastodon and what it was doing to his harvester. He claims it was the first time he drank in his life.

"Maloney claimed that if it was a mastodon that flattened Brown's harvester and not an alien on a pogo stick, it was only balancing nature.

"Brown said his harvester was totaled and set its value at over two million dollars.

"Maloney assured Brown that he would be compensated—if it were proved it was a mastodon. A solution would be forthcoming.

"Brown asked what would be done.

Maloney replied, 'We'll reintroduce the sabre-tooth tiger.'"

The sad shroud over this controversy is that there may be a solution to this problem, yet the government has let it pass: The Forest Service—in these hard economic times, just pulled 350 cattle guards. Why were they pulled when the same government is applying a stimulus package? These positions should immediately be reinstated, retrained and returned to work as "wolf guards."

So I look at the rising moon and it all makes me wonder. Do I want a government that says one thing while it does another? Do I want wolves in my corrals? Do we really need Brittany Spears? Rush Limbaugh? My cheeks are starting to itch. Every full moon I go through this same damn thing. Shaving is impossible. I hate shaving. I'm itching all over. I smell mint jelly. I gotta get some lamb.

OWW WWWUUUuuuuuuuuuuuuuuuu

I hear a helicopter.

# PASSIONATE GROANS AND BROKEN BONES

When the python falls in love

He does so with a crush.

Not the way you're thinking of

But still, it'd make you blush

MOM

DAD

# 4

# SHUTTING THE DOOR

**F**or the third time this morning they have left the back door open. They've gone outside inadequately dressed again. They haven't picked up their room for two days. I can't tell them anything. I even caught them swearing. They are always late. They have an attitude. Parents.[1] They just are not the same these days.

Mine just paid me a visit. My dad is 86 and has pulmonary fibrosis. On oxygen, he knows his time is more limited than ever. My mom, 84, is in perfect health. Not a gray hair on her head. But she has memory problems, a polite way of saying Alzheimer's.

It saddens me because I want to tell them things that we all want to tell our parents but can't because they are our parents and this is real life and such things don't come out easy. I have this rough draft letter that's gone around in my head now for 30 years. I have never sent it.

> Dear Mom and Dad,
>
> I'm sorry for not writing you sooner. Don't worry, I am not asking for money, or for anything else. I just wanted to tell you how grateful I am for my upbringing and for your patience with me in my formative years. All those things you tried so hard to train me to do I now actually do. I automatically pick up my room and make my bed. I don't snack between meals and I no longer swipe cookie dough when someone is baking. I am punctual and I even expect other people to be. I dress appropriately for all occasions and weather. I don't leave outside doors open. You remember, Dad? "Bloody" was your description of open doors. It was the one swear word mom would let you get away with in front of us kids. It was only used in one sentence: "Shut the bloody door!"
>
> There are deeper things I wish to tell you, like in high school at Halloween when you, Mom, found all those smashed eggs in my pocket and I refused to talk, but one of my buddies broke and spilled the beans admitting

---
[1] R.I.P.

we'd been caught by the police who'd smashed all the eggs in our pockets and let us go. There was also the night of "Hitler's revenge" when seven of us with Volkswagen bugs went downtown and surrounded the richest cars we could find and escorted them across town without letting them turn. The police tried to arrest us but we all jumped out of our cars and they couldn't pin a specific driver to a specific car so they had to let us go—but you heard about it anyway. I think you thought it was funny, Dad, but you didn't show it. You, Mom, were certain that I was the next rebel without a cause.

And I really am sorry about that time in college when I took care of your house while you were on vacation—only you came home early. You couldn't even park near your own house because of all the people at the party. You walked in with everyone yelling "na-na-na-nah, heyyyy JUDE" to the blasting stereo. How can I ever apologize for putting you through that? I can only thank you for your tolerance and persistence. I could go on, but you get the point. I hope you can see all your efforts really did turn me into a normal, responsible human being.

Thanks, Mom. Thanks, Dad. I love you.

But I don't send it. When my parents are visitors in my house, I don't feel the sentimentality I do when they are elsewhere. Instead I see my bad traits, a reflection of who I am. Friends don't see these things, which is why they are friends.

For example, my Dad likes to go for drives. Only he insists on driving. God forbid if he meets another driver like himself. While cutting corners and running stop signs he tells me about his buddies who are dead and dying. Some he's known since high school. As they die off he keeps track of them as if he were collecting baseball cards. It's sad to think he might be last. Is this the same as knowing you have more cards than your friends?

On the other hand my mom only has vague ideas of who is left and who isn't. What she remembers are stories of her homestead childhood. They're entertaining stories unless you hear them repeated five times a day. Could this be karma for all those times on road trips when we kids sang songs like *99 Bottles Of Beer On The Wall* and wouldn't shut up? I'm surprised my parents made it this far.

Although my mom was adamant that, as a kid, I pick up my room, she currently is not picking up her room in my house. Yet, outside that room, she obsessively picks up everything else. She especially has it in for my shop. My shop is not messy but I do leave tools out for projects I'm working on. She is always picking up my tools and putting them away in places that are logical for her, but where only an archaeologist will someday find them.

As a pair, it is impossible to keep them out of trouble. Last year at Halloween, the cops were in their driveway at 2 a.m. pounding on the front door. They had spotted a "Slow children" road sign in their driveway that an 80-something geriatric prankster had planted there. What the police thought my parents were doing and what they expected to find I don't know, because my dad slept through their visit, flashing lights and all. However, they did manage to get my mom up. Apparently my mom has a selective memory because in the morning, although she forgot what she told the police, she remembered the intrusion. She drove down to the station without getting lost and gave them an additional piece of her mind. I am dreading a future phone call for bail money.

So although I would really like to write that letter to them I am first going to post some rules for their next visit.

# RULES FOR YOUR NEXT VISIT!

☞ 1) Pick up your room. That way you won't lose the pills you're supposed to take.

☞ 2) Stay out of the kitchen. I know you wish to help, Mom, but you could help more by staying away—especially from those on/off stove and oven dials you so randomly like to rotate. Insurance is not cheap these days.

☞ 3) Dad, when you drive, SLOW DOWN. Stop still means stop. It doesn't mean yield. Same with red lights. And turn your blinker off!

☞ 4) Are you dressed adequately? The Depression has been over for almost 70 years.

☞ 5) Measurements of time continue to be the same. Clocks still keep the same time. Consult your watch. I know you are retired but there are people in this world who aren't.

☞ 6) Under no circumstances are you to play "Hey, Jude" on the piano or on any other instrument in this household even if it was brought in.

☞ 7) **SHUT THE BLOODY DOOR!**

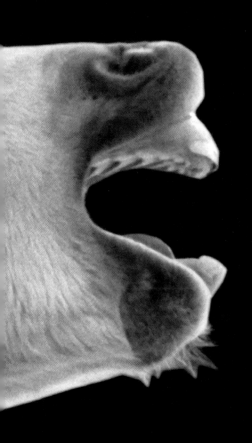

# SEASONED GREETINGS

Standing on a sage

Not wearing any cloves

Aren't you rather chili?

Only Oreganos.


Too many seasons in a year

Is that the way it goes?

Does thyme hold you at bay?

Only Oreganos.

CHAPTER

# 6

# I DIDN'T SAY THAT!

**I**f you think technology will save us, think again. My voice recognition program refuses to recognize me. I've told it a thousand times my name is Whit but always it calls me "with." Sure it boasts a bag of words but it scatters their phonetic sounds like Johnny Appleseed on a broadcasting mission. It even knows the word "grammar" but has no idea of its meaning, let alone its context. It joins words with unscrupulous abandon. It pledges allegiance to no one or no concept. For example, take the Pledge of Allegiance. As if there isn't enough controversy surrounding this issue here is my unprincipled monster's rendition weighing in:

*Pledge allegiance to the flagging United States of America into the puppets for which stands one nation ignited flirting justice for all.*

For me this poses a dilemma. I use my voice recognition program because I have Parkinson's and I am losing my ability to type. But what I say is not what shows up on the screen. Am I responsible for this? What if Homeland Security gets hold of my hard drive?

Yet there is no use trying to attach headings onto its amoral compass. It is technology run amuck. It's not that voice recognition doesn't possess its own HAL-like personality. But nothing is sacred. It even annihilates the Ten Commandments, which I best not divulge here other than to say that with a wry humor it renders "*Thou shalt not commit adultery*" into "*Michelle recommended only.*" The only thing it doesn't give me is her phone number.

**IT TURNS WILLIAM WORDWORTH'S "DAFFODILLS" INTO "DATA BILLS."**

And what about poetry? Voice recognition knows no beauty. It turns William

WHIT WITH WHIT

Wordworth's "*Daffodils*" into Data Bills while Tennyson's "*Light Brigade*" charges "Happily happily happily onward." And not even a sadistic bonsai artist could twist Joyce Kilmer's "*Trees*" in such an unseemly manner. It's poetry guaranteed to bring tears to the eyes, although not the usual kind. Here's my computer's collaborated version:

*I think that I shall never see*
*Up one lovely as a tree*
*A tree is hungry mouth is pressed*
*Against your sweet flowering breast*
*A tree that lets it go all day*
*And left her leafy arms to pray*
*The tree that may in summer where*
*Vannesa Robbins in her hair*
*Bond is blossoming snow inflamed*
*Linda Bentley lives with rain*
*Paul Miller made fools like me*
*But only God can make a tree*

I haven't a clue who Vannesa Robbins, Linda Bentley or Paul Miller might be other than prodigy of genetic and computer codes breeding unchecked in some programmer's basement. Certainly not someone wholesome like Julie Andrews who although she might perfectly enunciate, would only have her words slaughtered through this evil technological advancement. So what chance do people with foreign accents and speech impediments have? Can you imagine the modern remake of *My Fair Lady*? Eliza Doolittle would have smoke streaming from the computer's portals, hurricanes would blow Spain's rain from here to breakfast until Professor Higgins would at last address the screen with a cricket bat shortly before losing it altogether and going on a random killing spree.

And yet some days the program acts better than others. Just last week it almost dictated a letter perfectly. That is until I got to the end. I signed off, "Best Regards, Whit."

Only it didn't call me Whit. As usual, it called me "with."

So I said, "I said Whit!"

And it displayed, "I said With."

I yelled: "I said, Whit, dammit!"

"I said with dammit," it replied.

"Whit Whit Whit!" I screamed.

**WHIT WHIT WHIT! I SCREAMED.**

"With with with," read the screen.

"Words," I thought, hyperventilating. "They are only words." I needed to relax. Calm down. Go read. I picked up *Alice in Wonderland*.

THINKING OF NOTHING

I am too old to be sitting here like a pretzel because that French girl wasn't eaten—the uneaten French girl I met in France (a likely place to meet a French girl). She told me a story of sailing the Atlantic with her boyfriend. When they came to the Canary Islands, she wanted to sail to Africa; he wanted to return home to the U.S. They broke up. He sailed on alone. Two days out his boat went down; he drifted on a life raft for 76 days. She only learned of his ordeal after he was rescued. He wrote a million-copy bestseller. She wrote him a letter. Traveling to New York she visited him. She imagined him still skinny; he was anything but and he couldn't stop eating. He told her she wouldn't have made it on the raft because he would've had to eat her. I only relate the story because if he had eaten her, adding cannibalism on top of his incredible survival, his books sales would have doubled and I wouldn't be here sitting like a pretzel. Now that scenario might be happening in a parallel universe but not this one. In this one I get Parkinson's, meet the uneaten French girl who advises me that to tame my disease I really should learn to meditate.

The last time I attended any group self-improvement

program was EST in 1976. In Latin, EST is "to be." "Conned" should have followed it. It was the brainchild of a vacuum cleaner salesman who randomly plucked and plagiarized aphorisms and ideas everywhere from Buddhism to Freud. Half-baked, packaged and sold like Amway, it was delivered with the sensitivity of a train wreck.

Really, I'm not cynical; it's just that cults, religions and flavor-of-the-day encounter groups have the same effect on me as chalk screeching on a blackboard. I think of the Hari Krishnas and Rashneesh as organized lunacy that gave not only Eastern religion a bad name but humanity as well. Meditation outfits I pigeonholed right in the same receptacle.

However, I was curious. Researching, I learned:

☞ 1) There are numerous forms of meditation and that they differ as zanily as Christianity's strange tangents;

☞ 2) Meditation should not be compared to religion nor is it a sect. However, it is a practice used in Buddhism just like what kneeling or guilt is to mackerel snapping;

☞ 3) Mowing the lawn and washing dishes do not qualify as previous meditation experience. Those are spouse-induced trances.

# VISPASSANA VISPASSANA VISPASSANA

Digging some more, one species caught my attention—Vipassana. Although it sounded more like a brand of dish soap or a motor scooter, Vipassana is, or so the web claimed, one of the original and purest forms of meditation, no icon, no word or words to repeat, just simple breathing. It sounded so easy. But what I really liked was the price. For a ten-day session the cost was what I felt like. I signed on.

**DAY ONE.** So here I am, almost an hour into a ten-day commitment of learning and practicing meditation but all it is helping do so far is cripple me. I am in the meditation hall. A taped chant begins. Maybe it's background noise to mask the groans and wailings that are about to start from everyone folded into the lotus position. And if their legs are throbbing as bad as mine, knowing they will never ever function again, the wailing should start any minute now. My ligaments and tendons feel like old rubber bands stretched to the max being heated by a torch.

But the wails never start, although there is perpetual shuffling going on. Next to me is a longhaired redhead who, if he moved any more, I'd call it a dance. But I can't open my eyes to watch. I'm not allowed to while meditating, or at least trying to meditate. I am supposed to be concentrating on breathing through my nose; apparently I can't do this with my eyes open. Outside the meditation hall for the next 10 days, I'm not allowed to even make eye contact or speak with anyone except with

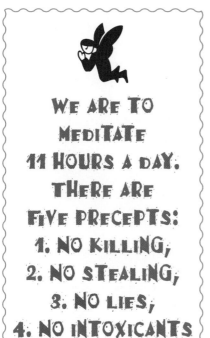

WE ARE TO
MEDITATE
11 HOURS A DAY.
THERE ARE
FIVE PRECEPTS:
1. NO KILLING,
2. NO STEALING,
3. NO LIES,
4. NO INTOXICANTS
5. AND NO SEX.

the teacher at specific times if I have a question. We (about 40 people) are to maintain not only silence but noble silence—whatever that is—for the entire duration. We are to meditate 11 hours a day; three of those hours being mandatory supervised in the meditation hall, the other hours can be in the meditation hall or in our rooms. There are five precepts: no killing, no stealing, no lies, no intoxicants and no sex. (Too bad, some of my best sex has been with myself.) Half the 40 are women. They're separated from us, sleep in another dorm, eat in a separate dining room, and meditate on the other side of the meditation hall. As for rules: no leaving the course before it's over, no outside communication, no reading and no writing, not even notes.

Ready for disability, I make it to the break. I feel like a mummy trying to stand. I hobble outside trying to get my legs to trust me again. For breaks we are given a small pasture contained within the hedgerow of blackberries and other bushes. I am barefoot and the grass is soothing. The pasture is mowed in grids creating 16 squares. The women have a separate walking area. Myself and my other fellow male meditators shuffle amongst the paths. Heads down, everyone is pensive and contemplative, taking slow steps. Apparently this breathing through the nose is some heavy stuff. We must look like the diurnal version of the *Night of the Living Dead*.

And then it happens. I can't explain it because I too am looking down, looking pensive, and I don't see it. I trod on a slug the size of a banana. I have just broken number one precept. I have just murdered a slug. Okay, involuntary slug slaughter. . . . Do you know what is in a slug? The same on the inside as on the outside only more of it, and there it is all smeared on the bottom of my foot like a mixture of Brussels sprouts, Vegemite, and Barry Manilow lyrics. What happens now? Will this keep me forever from reaching enlightenment? With such guilt on my mind and a slimed slug on my foot, I return to the meditation hall.

Continuing, through my knots of pain, a recorded Indian voice tells me as it's told me all day to breathe softly through my nose and think of nothing. Just breathe through my nose, feeling the sensation. No other details given. Observe the air going

in and out of my "nose-trils," the voice repeats "Feel it in your left nose-tril, now your right nose-tril, now both your nose-trils." And think of nothing.

How can I think of nothing? If I think of nothing isn't nothing something? And what about the active volcano we are sitting under that might blow up any minute? What's the protocol then? While everyone is getting the heck out of Dodge we are to sit here calmly while hot ash fills up our nose-trils? Years from now, like Pompeii, they will dig us up all sitting there calmly in rows like terra-cotta soldiers. How do I stop thinking?

# I HAVE SEXUAL FANTASIES

**DAY TWO.** Like yesterday morning a gong awakens me. I'm not hit in the head with it but it being four in the morning I might as well be. There is no breakfast. We are to be in the meditation hall by 4:30. Yesterday morning there was a rugby scrum in the meditation hall foyer at the shelf stuffed with pillows and blankets and kneeling blocks. Most of these people had done the course before. They grabbed all the best pillows. Inside the hall we are to sit on our assigned two-foot square padded cushion. On each space everyone has carefully built his or her nest of pillows either to sit or kneel on. Most people easily collapse down into their lotus position, shuffle their pillows into optimum comfort and pull their blankets over them shawl-like as they settle in to meditate. I crumple into my lotus position like a failed erection collapsing.

Today I try kneeling. The meditation begins. Kneeling proves just as painful. The pain, new and different, is like kneeling on a hot grill. So I can't even imagine what metaphor the redhead next to me is feeling. Having an even tougher time than yesterday, he squirms nonstop as if tied naked on a nest of red ants.

And with the pain I am supposed to think of nothing? Ignoring the fact I begin to think of other things, I argue with people I dislike. Thanks to the home-court advantage of my brain, I always win. I begin writing a novel.

"Whit Deschner has written another brilliant piece of work seizing all the elements of a classic: bigotry, bigamy, polygamy, verbosity, parity, parody, a matrixed plot, and enough foreshadowing to shade an entire city."

I have sexual fantasies. Another argument. "What time is it?"

Distantly the voice tells me, "Breathe naturally through your nose-trils. Feel the air moving. Your right nose-tril, now your left nose-tril…"

I return to my novel, ignoring the fact that my knees have come off the grill and are now being worked on by the IRA, which is busy drilling holes into my kneecaps.

"Breathe naturally."

There. No thoughts. Wait! What's this? A booger the size of an asteroid has lodged itself in my left nose-tril. Now what? I panic, breathing faster. How do I get it out of there? Where do I dispose of it? I must leave it there. What happens if one clogs my right nose-tril? They will see me breathing through my mouth. I won't really be meditating, which I'm not anyway. Breathing through my mouth, I wonder what the penalty is? Surely I'm headed for trouble. Think of nothing.

But I can think of nothing but that booger clogging that left nostril that is keeping me from the Enlightenment that no doubt lies just to the other side of it.

Do boogers contain DNA? Can you clone a person from one?

**DAY THREE.** You try it. Go on. Imagine nothing. No thoughts. Just nothing. Now try and think of nothing for five minutes without thinking of anything else. But you can't do it, can you? I sure wasn't getting anywhere. If only I had a screen and keyboard in front of me it would be easy. With writer's block I spend hours just thinking of nothing. In fact some writers like Gertrude Stein or James Michener made careers out of writing entire books of nothing.

I return to my old pattern to escape my pain; my thoughts are wandering rapidly again. Isn't this really all about kneeling and suffering pain to make other pain go away? Like smashing your thumb with a hammer just so it feels better after? I try to hide the pain; in order to do this I need the brains and body of a Gumby. My novel has grown increasingly complex. So much so that I forget completely what I cooked up yesterday so I begin again. If only I had a pen or pencil. . . . Reluctantly, trying to be good, I left my notebook and pen in the car—which is out of bounds—before the course started.

Today we learn that it is really not the breathing or my nose that I am to concentrate on; it is the small area under it—the one about the size of mustaches that were popular with German dictators in the late 1930s. I am to feel the skin in this stamp-sized area, feel a tingle, prickle, anything, just feel it. Feel the vibrations on it.

Okay I do. So this is meditating?

The weather is cool and walking within the prescribed area during a break I put on a coat and discover a pencil in my pocket! Being raised Catholic I already feel guilty just feeling its shape. I still need a piece of paper but already in my mind I have sinned. I have probably been blacklisted anyway for killing a slug so what's the problem breaking a rule to write a few notes?

Going back to my bunk I search the pockets in all my pants and find an old bank receipt. Now then, where can I go to jot some things down? And what will they do if they catch me? Make me sit in lotus position for one hour without moving? Besides, everyone in my dorm room has already broken the rule of noble silence. They talk liberally in their sleep; not just talking but having entire conversations punctuated liberally with farts. Besides, I'm just going to write key words not really notes. Resisting everything but the temptation I slip into one of the toilet stalls and jot words.

**DAY FOUR.** Lotus position, kneeling, it doesn't matter what position. I'm not made out to be a monk. I see someone else now sitting in a chair and ask if I can have one too. There much better! However the space next to me is empty. The redhead kid is gone. Did they disappear him for making too much distracting shuffling noise? Maybe he hung himself in the night. Maybe he escaped.

"Feel the sensations," the voice is telling me. Where was I? What's he talking about?

# I WISH THAT FRENCH GIRL HAS BEEN EATEN!

**DAY FIVE.** Somewhere I missed something. That little patch below the nose I was to move to the top of my head and create the same sensitivity there. And from there I was to spread the sensation down my body, part by part. "Feel the sensations. Any sensation, gross or small," the voice says. My arm is shaking from the Parkinson's. My back is now seizing up. And I have to fart. Does that count?

Today, and from here on out, we are to sit each meditation for a full hour without moving. We have reached the point where the torturer can no longer render pain to the tortured. I am beginning to think of this as prison or being at church or, worse still, a prison service. However, I actually do last the entire hour without moving but not without extreme pain. Nevertheless, I wish that French girl had been eaten.

I am thankful for the walks, the short ones between sits and the long ones after meals. They have become an art. On the grid walk in the grass I try and always turn or go straight accordingly, trying not to pass anyone oncoming. It's sort of like playing human Pac Man. Everyone is doing it, although I hardly know who everyone is. Mostly I know them by their shoes. I think of them as fellow monks. Brothers. There is a brother out walking in front of me on my lane when a stranger happens onto the lawn. The stranger approaches him, asking for directions somewhere. Sworn to silence, the brother puts his finger in front of his mouth. The stranger shakes his head. Next the brother makes a zippered-lips imitation. The stranger steps back. The brother clasps his hand over his mouth. Another step back. The brother panics and begins wildly gesturing, like a malfunctioning semaphore, pointing this way and that. The stranger turns and all but runs back the way he came certain he just stumbled into the midst of a lunatic asylum where someone left the lobotomy ward door open.

**DAY SIX.** The three mandatory meditations are started and ended with chants by the head Mucky Muck, S.N. Goenka, the teacher who returned Vipassana to India from Burma after it had been lost for centuries. It is Goenka's recorded voice that has been telling me the last six days to breathe through my nose-trils and to feel the sensations of on my skin. Daily, his chants grow longer. At first they were unsettling as his voice sounds more like that of a gut-shot gunfighter lying in the hot sun, dying, muttering unintelligible directions to where he buried the money. He makes Tom Waits sound like Rod Stewart, well okay, maybe Joe Cocker. He's not Little Richard anyway.

Actually, I would prefer a Gregorian chant. At least they had a tune and their timing was pretty good, too. It should be. After all they figured out the calendar. I wonder if the Julians chanted? They sure couldn't get their calendar right. Come to think more about it, I would really prefer Aretha Franklin. Or some good old gospel music, say, Mahalia Jackson. Sometimes Goenka's chants spill out words almost familiar, like Frank Sinatra singing "*My Way*." Am I hallucinating?

That night after everyone has turned into their bunks I am tempted to say, "Goodnight, John Boy." The more I think of saying such things and the more I can't talk, the funnier everything seems. Would they reprimand me? Would people laugh? Am I going nuts here?

**DAY SEVEN.** I'm not sure what others are feeling as we're being told to feel every little piece of our skin. Any sensation. I still don't know if a fart counts. We are given two meals a day, breakfast at 6: 30 and lunch at 11. For dinner we are given a piece of fruit. Obviously one doesn't come here to eat. The food is strictly vegetarian. Lots of beans and rice, but tofu is the featured item. I'm not sure where tofu ever came from but can't they think of anything better to do with it than eat it? Can't they put it in air bags? Wouldn't that be a surprise? I wonder what the vegetarian equivalent is of the Heimlich maneuver? Don't people ever gag on tofu?

Because of the food, I am one huge windbag and walking is of no use trying to secretly release so much gas. But what I can't figure out is that recently, in the meditation hall, there's perfect silence, just the occasional cough. Why hasn't someone released the big one? It would be all the funnier if it came from the women's side.

And if I did it would I be reprimanded?

*"Brother Whit, breaking wind in the meditation hall is the ultimate breaking of noble silence. You are sentenced to walk 40 laps in the walking area self-flatulencing yourself the entire distance."*

But silence is maintained. It must be what the pillows are really for. Tibetan mufflers.

**DAY EIGHT.** I'm not sure where to draw the line between religion and prison as both prisoners and monks live in cells—optimum space for meditating—nor can you expect much from the meals. As I walk silently around I begin to think of this area as a botanical prison yard. There is nothing to stop me from walking away, just my own prison walls I built when I agreed to come here. Still I can't help thinking of Dachau, Stalig 13, or was it 17? Sing Sing. Steve McQueen.

I am thinking of leaving. I can sit the hour without moving and little pain. But I am nowhere near a meditative state unless a meditative state means the pain I caused myself from sitting here trying to meditate.

I'm thirsty. I think of Gunga Din and further know that I'm really losing it because I'm wondering, "Was Gunga Din a hydrocephalic?"

**DAY NINE.** Having to avoid eye contact with everyone in the last nine days I am almost afraid to look at my own image in the mirror, scared that it too will look away from me.

Today's the last serious day. I don't feel any closer to enlightenment. My mind wanders. What if Medusa met St Patrick? This amusement soon dissolves into frustration. Concentrating on not concentrating, I did feel champagne bubbles issuing from the top of my head but to get them to spread over my body has not worked. Is this Karma? Is it holding me back because I jotted down notes on napkins and scraps of paper, notes that will be unintelligible anyway?

The teacher has warned us not to think in metaphors describing any sensations that we might have, like champagne bubbles, as it plants ideas in others' heads of what they should feel. But that afternoon I feel another metaphor; suddenly, but only for a few minutes, my body feels electric. As soon as I'm consciously aware of it though, it disappears and refuses to come back. Outside during break I feel exhausted, as if I have gone through a major operation.

## I'M AFRAID TO HEAR MY OWN VOICE.

**DAY TEN**

**WE CAN TALK,**
**MAKE EYE CONTACT,**
**CONVERSE, BUT:**
**1. NO TOUCHING,**
**2. NO SEX,**
**3. NO STOLEN BEER,**
**4. NO KILLING**
**OR LYING**
**5. AND NO SEX.**

**DAY TEN.** Today we can talk once again. We can make eye contact and hold conversations. However, we can't touch, have sex, drink stolen beer, kill, or lie about any of it.

I'm afraid to hear my own voice.

Trying to match people's shoes with their faces is almost impossible. There is a vernacular going around, almost cult-like. People are saying, "That was an awesome course." "Did you have a good sit?" And, as one brother said to me, "It was great sitting with you!" I looked at his shoes. I swore I'd never seen them before, let alone a stolen glance at his face. But I'm not being cynical or even skeptical. Now that it is over, it was a good course and I did have a good sitting, if that's what it was.

Later. Did it tame the Parkinson's? No. Did it help otherwise? Yes. I don't know why, but I don't care to. Do I continue to meditate? Yes, but I can't break the habit of wanting to slip into the bathroom, fart and jot notes.

# THE MOST DANGER- OUS CATCH

I was pushing the age when I was supposed to grow a beer belly and stoic opinions, but this brave, new territory greeted me instead with nose hairs and Parkinson's. Ten years later I have become, unwillingly, a Double Jeopardy wiz on the subject—Parkinson's that is; nose hairs I know nothing about. I didn't volunteer to be an expert. The disease volunteered me. I couldn't hide it. My storage pile of facts started with people asking me things like: "You're shaking. Are you cold?"

"Nope."

"Nervous?"

"Nope."

No one ever continues. They suddenly know it's a place they wish they hadn't trod.

## "Parkinson's."

This has always produced a string of apologies; then soon their inquisitiveness kicks in, the part I like, for suddenly I am fielding PD-related questions like, "Say, Whit, what's the J stand for in Michael J Fox's name anyway?" "Jeronimo." Or, "What was Mohammad Ali's name before he changed it?" "Lou Alcindor." Sometimes people even ask me frivolous things like, "Does Parkinson's lead to dementia?" "Of course not." (I wrote this didn't I?) Or,

## "Just what is Parkinson's?" And, "How do we get it?"

# PARKINSON'S IS A CHRONIC "NEURODEGENERATIVE DISORDER" WHICH IS CONFUSING BECAUSE THAT SUMS UP LIFE IN GENERAL.

Parkinson's is a *chronic neurodegenerative disorder* which is confusing because that sums up life in general. So how *do* we get it? Experts insist we possess a genetic disposition towards Parkinson's catalyzed by an environmental toxin. This is, of course, just a polite way of saying we get it from toilet seats. I know this because I know the exact seat I got mine from. It was in an Alaskan fish camp that I used to commercial fish out of. I was trying to stabilize the world, hugging the above-mentioned seat while jettisoning six tequila sunrises consumed in an undiscerning manner. I was young and the experience was good for me because I know how bad I felt afterwards and it prepared me for the future. I'll admit I was pretty down being diagnosed with Parkinson's but not half as bad as I felt after throwing up six sunrises. By comparison though, and despite the false notion of impending dementia, Parkinson's is still not a fun disease to have. Fortunately, people are concerned. They look at me with uncut sympathy and ask, "Have you seen that TV show, *The Deadliest Catch?*"

Being a commercial fisherman, the onset of Parkinson's was certainly not welcome; not that having another occupation the onset would've been more warmly greeted. Other fisherman assured me that it was okay because I could still shake fish out of the nets and that all old fishermen become demented anyway. However, another Parkinson's trademark is an increasing loss of balance; I'd already gone overboard once without any disease's help, and once is enough. So I quit being a fisherman. The diagnosis was totally life-changing, the consequences paramount: I could no longer play pick-up sticks with the local kids. I pondered over new jobs. Becoming a neurosurgeon was out. Bomb diffusion? Not an option.

I felt no different than the armless Venus de Milo applying for a trapeze artist's position. But hey, I could shake paint or agitate DNA vials or shake Martinis, or I could shake packets of non-dairy creamer so they could be opened safely and not spilled over everything. I could sand wood. I could scramble eggs. I could train my tremor to knit. I could ring a bell at Christmas for donations. I could become a Morse code operator—although I knew I'd just repeat myself. There were also skills that I maintained, well, kind of: I could type an amazing 70 wpm, so long as they were the words "a" or "I." My handwriting was almost as fast as my typing, but as it started to shrink (another of PD's many outstanding features) people could no longer read what I wrote, including myself, but I never could anyway. I could fill in for a doctor filling out illegible prescriptions. In time I reverted to a computer voice recognition program—Dragon Naturally Speaking. (Call their support and their voice recognition experts neither recognize nor speak recognizable English.) So far nothing I've done trains it. (Where the hell is Saint George when he's needed?) Instead it helps me invent new languages that even a house-sized Rosetta boulder couldn't translate. I'm not dead in the water yet because between these skills I still can write articles where the word "could" appears 14 times in one paragraph.

And just because I compulsively count the number of "coulds" in a paragraph has nothing to do with dementia. Dementia has nothing to do with such compulsiveness. Compulsiveness has nothing to do with dementia. Nothing has compulsiveness to do with dementia. Dementia has compulsiveness to do nothing.

Fortunately, Parkinson's does not lead to dementia (not to say I am not already demended) and it's a much better disease to have than Alzheimer's: I'd rather spill half my drink than forget where I left the bottle. Unfortunately, Parkinson's is not something you take a couple of pills for and wake up in the morning feeling better. You take a couple of pills; you *still* wake up in the morning but you still have to take a couple more pills, then a couple more and a couple more and so on. Parkinson's does not kill you. *Eventually* you choke to death on all the pills you have to swallow, or try to. Fortunately, science and technology promise to save me.

There are especially complicated brain operations because they involve especially complicated parts with especially complicated names: thalamotomies for the thalamus, pallidotomies for the pallidum, lobotomies for all members of congress and deep brain stimulation (of the subthalamic nucleus) that can make you look normal even if you're not. The deep brain stimulation holds the most promise. It's an implanted, high frequency electrode that turns off targeted neurons in the subthalamic nucleus and is run by an electric fencer planted under your skin just below your funny bone. It's not yet as sophisticated as what Arnold Schwarzenegger had in *Terminator* that told him exactly what to say… but far more refined than what the speechwriters told Gov. Schwarzenegger to say. Actually, I'd like to know how he explained things to Maria.

THERE ARE ESPECIALY COMPLICATED BRAIN OPERATIONS BECAUSE THEY INVOLVE ESPECIALLY COMPLICATED PARTS WITH ESPECIALLY COMPLICATED NAMES.

# ANOTHER TRAIT ABOUT PARKINSON'S —MINE ANYWAY— IS YOU CAN'T LIE. IF I LIE MY HAND TREMOR INCREASES.

Unfortunately brain-intrusive operations are relatively new. Look at it this way: the year is 1492, your brain is America and your neurosurgeon's name is Columbus. You could end up like a pithed frog which, in Rush Limbaugh's case, would be an improvement—an "epithany" if you will. It won't be long though before the medical world gets them down pat and Walmart will be performing them while the oil is being changed in your car. Besides, I don't want an implant until it comes with an iPod option.

There's also locked hope in stem cell research, but the key is unavailable until the religious nutcakes come down with Parkinson's themselves. There is alternative research stealing stem cells from pigs, yet this would be the ultimate dilemma for a Jew or Muslim having pork cells embedded in their brains. At least they'd have something else to think about other than new nefarious ways to annihilate each other.

So what is Parkinson's really like to have? It's a nagging disease, like having your mother-in-law as your guardian angel. It's like going through your second puberty. Your voice changes and you become awkward. Freezing takes up a new meaning as does shaking hands. The shaking hand is just annoying; the freezing in place is frustrating. It does make me wonder, "What sort of ultimate and omnipotent creator would create a disease that makes a hand vibrate and then not give them somewhere to place the shaking hand in a socially acceptable manner?" I can't put my shaking hand in my pocket, nor can I sit and rest my hand in my lap. I sure can't rest it in the person's lap sitting next to me, say on a plane or bus or a park bench. And when I go to the theater I know exactly what people are thinking, "It's Pee-wee Herman!" As for the freezing? It is exactly that. The body freezes, except for the shaking. You want to move. You try to move. You think you're going to move. And then . . . nothing happens. The period standing there, doing nothing but shaking, waiting for a spring thaw, would be a great time to listen to the iPod implant.

Another trait about Parkinson's—mine anyway—is you can't lie. If I lie, my hand tremor increases. If I lie more, I begin to jackhammer. I now understand Pinocchio. So, to answer the question honestly, "No, I have not seen the TV show *The Deadliest Catch*." I must watch it because I used to fish with one of the show's skippers, Eric. In the summers Eric fished salmon out of the same fish camp I did. Early one season a wholesale screwball showed up in camp informing everyone he'd been sent as manager. He introduced himself as Burt and from then on he was known as Ernie. He never got the joke. He'd been given the combination to the safe to get the checks so the camp crew could get paid but, worried that someone would steal the code, he tore it into tiny pieces, ate it and immediately forgot it. The combination was sent via short wave radio for all Alaska to hear. Ernie got the job simply because he was Eric's neighbor. No one checked his references, like, say, to see if he was demented. For some reason Ernie lasted far longer that season than I ever thought he would. He lasted exactly until the night he broke out all the windows in the galley.

Although Ernie was a card-carrying whacko he was also a ladies' man—for the entire two of them in camp. Well, they were women anyway. Barely. The camp owner had finagled some deal with the Kodiak jail. I gave them a wide berth, but not Ernie. Ernie was jovial. One thing I noticed about Ernie was that one of his hands trembled. I only mentioned the women because at mug-up I overheard one of them ask, "Hey Ernie! You cold? You're shaking."

"No," he answered.

"Nervous?"

"Nope," he said and looked down at his hand, "It just started doing that."

Which explained one thing—especially when we discovered that he drank all the camp's supply of vanilla before breaking out the windows in the galley—Ernie, we figured, had the DTs and was trying to dry out. The next morning he was found draped over a toilet seat.

But today I'm not so sure Ernie did have the DTs. With what I know now I think Ernie was in his early onset Parkinson's stage because it was in that camp where I hugged that same toilet seat, ejecting six sunrises, and where, I am almost positive, I caught my deadliest catch, Parkinson's.

# VINI VIDI DA VINCI

Tell me, tell me, Mona Leeze

What's that expression you wear with ease?

I'm begging to know, I'm on my knees,

If you'd only tell me, won't you please!

Is your mouth glued shut with Mozzarella cheese?

Or is it filled with a thousand peas?

Do you have a case of fleas?

Are you chilled by a winter breeze?

Maybe you're about to sneeze!

I'll bet you drank some antifreeze!

So, please, won't you tell me, Mona Leeze

What's the expression you wear with such ease?

# 9

# WE CHOOSE OUR FRIENDS BUT NOT OUR DISEASES

If Mao Zedong, Adolf Hitler, Generalissimo Francisco Franco, Terry Thomas, Yasser Arafat, Margaret Bourke-White, Salvador Dali, Pope John Paul II, Deng Xiaoping, George Wallace, Vincent Price, Pierre Trudeau, Mo Udall, James Doohan, Charles Schulz and Johnny Cash were all at a dinner party, what would they have in common?

They'd all be dead.

Okay, but besides dead? Let me put it this way: you would be ill-advised to serve dinner (and especially red wine) to this lot on your best linen tablecloth because they all had Parkinson's. After exhausting the subjects of death and Parkinson's, the latitude of topics between guests probably would shrink. Perhaps you'd hear Salvador Dali and the Generalissimo delve into the merits of Picasso's Guernica; Mao Zedong and Hitler could discuss exciting new developments of genocide, then end

> YOU WOULD BE ILL-ADVISED TO SERVE DINNER (AND ESPECIALLY RED WINE) TO THIS LOT ON YOUR BEST LINEN TABLE-CLOTH.

up arm wrestling; Pope John Paul II and Deng Xiaoping could argue over who has more control over more people, the Pope rants about stem cells and Deng Xiaoping, who has never heard of them, wants to know how many dissidents you can detain in one; Terry Thomas and Vincent Price confer about each other's teeth configurations and why Terry's wouldn't lend themselves to vampirism; George Wallace, Pierre Trudeau and Yasser Arafat deliberate over the pros and cons of divided states; Mo Udall and James Doohan argue about the environmental concerns of mining dilithium crystals, Doohan maintaining it was the dilithium crystals that brought on his PD; Charles Schulz alone doodles on napkins and draws a shaky picture of Snoopy trying to sleep on his doghouse in what appears to be an earthquake. Margaret Bourke-White photographs this historic occasion only to discover she forgot to put film in her camera while Johnny Cash is having no problem strumming his guitar, but is missing the fingerings and sings about boys named Sue and Rings of Fire, a song about his hemorrhoids.

Actually, I was sorry I looked up such trivia, but having caught the disease I find myself doing such off-the-wall research. I wanted to check up on the company I was keeping and whether the disease made these people famous. I wasn't about to miss an aspect of an affliction that might propel me into eminence. But I was hoping for more inspirational people. Why couldn't people like Gandhi, Jesse Owens, Errol Garner or Walt Kelly be on the list? Why did Hitler and Mao Zedong have to be there? The only listed person I appreciate is James Doohan. Well, Scotty, really. How many times did Scotty nurse his dilithium crystals to perform above calling for the Enterprise to save the universe? This was far more than Mao Zedung or Hitler ever did for anyone.

> I WANTED TO CHECK UP ON THE COMPANY I WAS KEEPING AND WHETHER THE DISEASE MADE THESE PEOPLE FAMOUS. I WASN'T ABOUT TO MISS AN ASPECT OF AN AFFLICTION THAT MIGHT PROPEL ME INTO EMINENCE.

(Franco was no shining rose either.) All the PD list needed was Joe Stalin, Pol Pot, Idi Amin, Tamerlane and my 8th grade math teacher, Don Smith. Still, I asked, "Did Parkinson's help mold these people?" Fortunately the answer is "no," unless further research proves that Hitler's famed salute was actually dyskinesia. Nor do I doubt the Pope had any problem sprinkling holy water with his shaking hands. I suppose when I was diagnosed with PD over ten years ago, I should have been happy. I should still be happy. At least I didn't have something horrible like congenital warts, a bad case of warbles, herpes or the heartbreak of psoriasis. Still, I wish Hitler and Mao Zedong would go trouble some other disease's manifest, and stop giving the rest of us with PD an association with such scum bags.

Of course, before Parkinson's was formally identified, all sorts of inspirational people might have had the disease. Sort of like that Buddhist conundrum about a tree falling in the forest and if no one is there to hear it, does it make a sound? If the disease wasn't identified yet, did people really have it? The answer to both these questions is, "Who cares?"

History contains plenty of references to Parkinson's symptoms. Homer alludes to it, referring to a king who can no longer compete in athletic contests because his limbs are no longer steady nor his feet, and "neither do my arms, as they once did, swing light from my shoulders." The Bible gives several mentions of permanently bent men. It is little surprise that Shakespeare, who wrote everything there was to write, covers it also in *King Henry VI*, when Dick asks Lord Say, "Why dost thou quiver, man?" Lord Say replies, "It is the palsy, and not fear, provokes me."

## Other historical references include:

**304-250 BC. Greece.** Anatomist Erasistratus describes paralysis in people who suddenly stop walking and temporarily freeze in place. He also observes that people with a lisp have trouble pronouncing his name.

**25 BC to 50 AD. Rome.** Encyclopedist Aulus Cornelius Celsus, having nothing better to do, compiles eight books of medicines in which he advises that those who suffer tremor should exercise and eat whatever they want, but sexual activity is to be restricted. Restricted to what he doesn't say. However, should temptation prevail, the person should afterwards be rubbed with olive oil *by boys, not men.*

**40-90 AD.** Meanwhile back in **Greece**, physician, pharmacologist and botanist Pedanius Dioscorides writes a monumental herbal book and states that, among other things, beaver testes prepared with vinegar and roses are helpful for trembling and convulsions and for all diseases of the nerves, being either drank or anointed. Yuk.

**129-200 AD.** Yet another **Greek** physician, Galen, writes extensively on disorders of motor function, including palpitation, tremor, convulsion and shivering, distinguishing between forms of shaking of the limb on the basis of origin and appearance. Geriatrics, he notes, exhibit tremor because of a decline in their power to control the motion of their limbs. The key to overcoming tremor is to abolish the proximal cause, but for the aged, this is impractical. Besides the tremor, the afflicted has wild, wide open eyes, lies rigid in bed as if he were made of wood and also suffers constipation and certain psychiatric symptoms.

# LEONARDO DA VINCI WRITES IN HIS SECRET NOTEBOOKS THAT "YOU WILL SEE THOSE WHO MOVE THEIR TREMBLING PARTS, SUCH AS THEIR HEADS OR HANDS WITHOUT PERMISSION OF THE SOUL.

**850-900 AD. Damascus.** Christian physician, Yahya Ibn Sarafyun, pens two medical compilations and lists among his prescriptions for nervous diseases a complex salve of 35 ingredients including myrrh, cypress and frogs "for gout and palsy, and for those who have the tremors, and for all the pains which take place in the nerves."

**980-1037 AD. Persia.** Hotshot physician, Ibn Sina, discusses the numerous forms of motor unrest in his chapter on nervous disorders in the "Canon of Medicine." Besides bathing in mineral baths, he recommends a composite that includes the excretion of the anal gland of the beaver. Obviously he'd been reading Pedanius Dioscorides' book but translated beaver testes incorrectly. I can't imagine he would have been popular with his patients advising them to eat the ass-end out of a beaver.

**1452-1519 AD. Italy.** Leonardo da Vinci writes in his secret notebooks that "you will see those who move their trembling parts, such as their heads or hands without permission of the soul; (the) soul with all its forces cannot prevent these parts from trembling." Soon after he places ads in local papers for non-trembling poker-faced models.

**1616-1654 AD. England.** Botanist, herbalist, physician and astrologer Nicholas Culpeper recommends "the oil of winged ants and earthworms" to combat Parkinson-like symptoms. (Before Parkinson's was named, people just went around saying, "I've got Parkinson-like symptoms.")

**1706-1767 AD. France.** Francois Boissier de Sauvages de la Croix provides an unmistakable description of the disease calling it "Sclerotyrbe Festinans". It's a blessing this name didn't catch on. How many people would admit, let alone be able to say, "I've got Scleortyrbe Festinans Disease." Which brings us to . . .

**1755-1824 AD. London.** In 1817 Surgeon James Parkinson writes his famous "An Essay on the Shaking Palsy" and clinically nails almost every symptom of the disease. He did not name the disease. That came sixty years later when it was named by Jean-Martin Charcot.

**1825-1893 AD. France.** Jean-Martin Charcot becomes the founder of modern neurology. And thanks to neurology we now know special facts about Parkinson's that will hopefully prevent others from coming down with the disease. Facts such as:

# USEFUL FACTS!

☞ Eating fruit bats on Guam can lead to Parkinson's because the bats feed on cycad seeds which contain a potent neurotoxin.

☞ Seeds, too, are also guilty in Mumbai where the Parsi burn aspand seeds in a ritual to rid their kids of the evil eye. The poisoning effects of the smoke may save the kids from the evil eye and the parents from a big optometrist bill, but it is also guilty of providing the Parsi community with almost the world's highest prevalence of Parkinson's disease.

☞ Japan is the only country where there are more women with PD than men.

☞ If you're a redhead you have twice the risk of developing the disease.

☞ Bulgarian Gypsies are almost immune to the disease, however, the study doesn't account for the fact that most Bulgarian Gypsies never live long enough to get Parkinson's.

So, if you are a red-headed Bulgarian Gypsy female living in Japan who likes roasting Guamese fruit bats over Aspand seeds and don't drink lots of coffee, don't smoke and have a low a cholesterol level, chances are Ray Stevens is going to write a song about you.

Obviously there are some precautions I never took regarding the above—along with some other people I've asked to dinner tonight: Muhammad Ali, Michael J Fox, Janet Reno, the Rev. Billy Graham and, Ozzy Osbourne . Ozzy even prepared the meal: Cornish game hens that he personally bit the heads off of. Right now I hear Rev. Billy telling Ozzy, "You know Black Sabbath was never the same without you." This could be an interesting evening. I look at everyone and realize the latitude of Parkinson's victims. I raise my glass and toast, "You can pick your friends, but you can't pick your diseases." Everyone raises their glasses and . . . spills their wine.

# BURNING LOVE

He was a narcissist

With a touch of arsonist

Who was burnt by his own desire

For he was cremated

By the love he created

Setting his heart on fire

# UNTIDALED

Blinded with emotion
She went down to the ocean
To where the cliffs are extremely steep
And there she wept
Then finally leapt
At a place called, "Lover's Leap."

But while doing her pouting
The tide took to outing
And now the tour guides do show
Where lost love and gravity
Made a large cavity
Far, far on the beach below.

# LiTTLe JACK R.I.P.

Little Jack Horner

Was sent to the coroner

Obviously strangled to death.

But the coroner with his thumb

From Jacks mouth pulled a plum

And said, "T'was this which robbed him of breath."

# IS YOUR GOOSE COOKED?

*(A ruling throne gathers no goose)*

Little Miss Muffit

Sat on a tuffit*

Eating Mother Goose.

Along came Spiderman

And sat down beside her and Slurped up all of the juice.

*there were no chairs

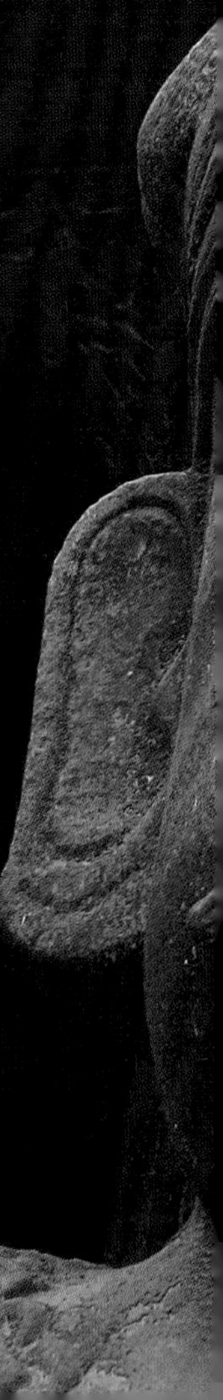

# LINGERING
# LING COD

Grasped in the fish monger's fingers

The lingering ling cod now lingers

Knowing in the fingers of the fish monger

A ling cod will linger no longer.

BACK BY THE

# NUMBERS

# CHAPTER 10

According to the 23andMe Genetic research lab there are a number of seemingly unrelated conditions and traits that are actually associated with Parkinson's. Personality traits including; being more agreeable, (I agree) but also people afflicted tend to be more neurotic and anxious, less extraverted and prefer sweet foods over salty ones. (Reluctantly I also agree.) The researchers even discovered that those with Parkinson's were less likely to have sky-dived or had liposuction.[1] Unfortunately, the links don't stop there. They include associations with back pain and joint replacement surgery, both of which occur more frequently in people with Parkinson's. I know. I'm a shining statistic. Let me tell you about it.

PATIENT #37217'S ACCOUNT

Two years ago I ordered a part for a project that I selfishly figured deserved priority attention—especially since I had to prepay ($147) Rob who took care of ordering special orders. When I returned two days later to fetch my special part, the store said my special part had come in; someone had seen it but didn't know where they'd seen it. I'd have to talk to Rob in Special Orders because he had special ordered it and Rob wasn't in."When's he coming back?"

---

[1] Surely, these researchers, researching themselves drawing lines between such a bizarre set of dots, will ultimately link themselves to discovering they are all descendants of The Little Rascals or that they all belong to Oprah's Book Club.

"Haven't a clue. He keeps special hours."

When Rob did return seven days later I thanked him for his expediency and for letting me know he was taking a vacation. Now my project was hopelessly behind.

"Having open heart surgery is no vacation," he answered.

Trying to save what was suddenly my reddening face, I tried consoling him. I told him I had Parkinson's.

"Got that too," he replied. I thought, "With that luck you ought to play the lottery."

Dealing with PD was annoying enough but another disorder stacked on top of that? God may work in mysterious ways, but he doesn't have to be a jerk about it. I felt lucky. Nevertheless, I was still irritated about my delayed part.

In time—1½ years—I finished my project. Meanwhile my luck was waning, and filling the void came a searing pain that started in my right hip and shot down my right leg. Usually I could readjust my position to alleviate the growing discomfort. "Sciatica." people said. It sounded like a prison in New York. Progressively the pain worsened. Finally I made an appointment with my doctor.

"Where would you rate the pain?" the nurse asked as she ushered me down the hall.

"In your office." She didn't laugh and probably jotted, "Not to be taken seriously. Most likely is trying to get prescription pain meds."

She took me into the examining room, took my coat, then my vitals, and pointed to a chart on the wall: happy face was 1; Japanese torture face was 10. "On this scale of 1 to 10, 10 being the highest, what's your pain level right now?"

I thought, "One to 10? What is this the Olympics? "One to 10?" she repeated. I looked at the chart.I tallied the score in my head: 1.5 for the lower back, 3 for the pain shooting down my right leg, and 1.5 for the numbness in my toes. "Six," I announced.

## THE WONG & BAKER PAIN SCALE

| | |
|---|---|
| 0-1 | No pain |
| 2-3 | Mild pain |
| 4-5 | Discomforting - moderate pain |
| 6-7 | Distressing - severe pain |
| 8-9 | Intense - very severe pain |
| 10 | UNBEARABLE PAIN |

"The doctor will be right in," she answered giving me a #3 you're-a-mild-pain look. Right in was half an hour. While waiting I looked at the pain gauge and wondered if despot nations used the Wong and Baker scale while torturing dissidents. How could Guantanamo even function without it? Then I thought of the Olympics, the old Olympics, not the BC Greek ones but the good vs. evil ones, the free world vs. the communists. We knew evil because Jim McKay made it clear how all the judged events with eastern-bloc Commies on the judging panel awarded soaring undeserved marks to their kindred comrades while doling out basement scores to our poor amateur red-blooded American athletes. Jim failed to mention the blood was doped.

**DOCTOR $96**

My doctor entered—$96—and I suddenly felt old, realizing he wasn't even born yet during those Olympics. And he was going to advise me.

"You'll need to get an MRI," he said. "We can try a lumbar epidural steroid injection. But surgery is probably what we're looking at." Not liking his clever use of *we* I first tried physical therapy—$186. The pain didn't lessen but grew worse. I began to walk like the depiction of the hunched over Cro-Magna Carta Man evolving to Upright-Modern Day-Investment-Banker-Man—only I was going backwards. I was going down. By the week's end I had descended almost completely to the carpet. My numbered pain was edging into an 8. I got the MRI—$2,199.75.

**P.T. $186**

**MRI $2,199.75**

I heard nothing from my doctor or the radiologist, but, still unwilling to go under the knife, I opted for the epidural injection, a syringe full of steroids.

The anesthesiologist who gave the injection—$2,542.36—said he wasn't good at interpreting MRIs but did say that the way he saw it, his needle "might" not work.

It didn't, but the procedure would have made a good alibi that Barry Bonds should have used. Subsequently, the pain was like having an invisible electric cage around me that was never static, and each time I tried to move I kept hitting its confines where it zapped and punished me. Some jolts I could bust through but others peeked into Japanese 10 torture, and I would instantly retract back to the lesser number which at least seemed more tolerable. Meanwhile the surrounding cage was growing smaller.

**INJECTION $2,542.36**

Trying to stand, fire shot down my leg. I began crawling around the house getting rug burns my knees, seeing the world from a dog's view, and thinking, "Good thing I'm not up to humping peoples' legs." God help me should I have gotten fleas because the pain level would have gone off the scale to scratch them. Bypassing any referrals, I made an appointment with a back specialist—$632.

**SPECIALIST $632**

Now if you're an explorer or a card player or a scientist or into S and M, the word "interesting" is a great word, but in the medical vernacular, when the charming professional looking at your MRI and freshly-shot x-rays—$254—exclaims with a smile, "interesting," hang on because "interesting" is not great. It's bad. But with the pain now a solid 9 she could have said, "We're sorry, Mr. Deschner, but we're going to have to cut off your head," and I wouldn't have cared. The good thing about "interesting" is that it got me promoted to the top of the operating list. I couldn't wait. The pain was so convincing even the Romanians

**X-RAY $254**

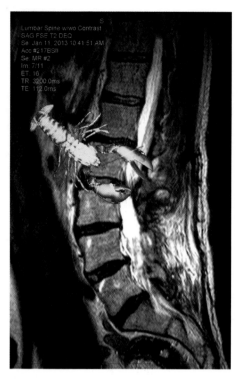

Lumbar Spine w/wo Contrast
SAG FSE T2 DEO
Se Jan 11 2013 10 41 51 AM
Acc #217BSII
Se MR #2
Im 7/11
ET 16
TR 3200.0ms
TE 112.0ms

and the East Germans would've given me high scores. Within 48 hours I was under the knife.

First though, I had to check in. All I can say is it took far less signing for Japan to surrender than it does to check into a hospital these days. I was handed a stack of papers to sign, and the registrar expertly flipped through them saying, "Here, here, here," several dozen times. I have no idea what I signed. Perhaps I forfeited my firstborn child—news to me—or I'm soon to become an indentured servant in Moldavia. I didn't care. I just wanted to get on with the operation. They fastened a bar code bracelet around my wrist and wheeled me into the Pre-Op Room. It became apparent that I had relinquished any and all dignity because I was immediately disrobed and given a hospital gown. Ridiculous hardly describes them. No one has a clue where these came from or what their purpose is. And it's to be worn backwards. Fig leaves would be far more dignified. Or an extra-large rolled pizza dough would have fit better and have been far more fashionable. Botched operations would just look like toppings. The best explanation I can think of is that gowns were developed to humiliate patients and encourage them to stay in bed. I'm surprised the airlines don't make passengers wear them. Easy for security, and people would remain seated for the duration of the flight.

As they wheeled me about, various people asked me who I was and what I was doing there. It was worse than philosophy class. I wanted to say, "I'm René Descartes. Je pense donc je suis[2]"; "Aristotle. I just consumed hemlock, and I'm here to have my stomach pumped"; "I'm Bill Bailey, and I want to go home"; "I'm Sylvester Stallone, and I

> IT BECAME APPARENT THAT I HAD RELINQUISHED ANY AND ALL DIGNITY BECAUSE I WAS IMMEDIATELY DISROBED AND GIVEN A HOSPITAL GOWN.

---

[2.] Translated: *Cogito ergo sum.*

am getting a sex change"; "I'm Tamerlane, and I am here with the sensitivity encounter group"; "Name's Whit Deschner, and I'm here for my lobotomy"; "The name is Bond, James Bond . . . "

Then the surgeon introduced himself and told me how he was going to carve me—$9,191—shave some excess bone off and graft it to the three vertebrae that he planned to fuse together with titanium screws and plates. It was four days away from Halloween, and I wondered if he ever carved pumpkins. And wouldn't that be a shock if he cut me open and I was full of pumpkin seeds?

**CARVING $9,191**

"We're going to put you under now, Mr. Deschner."

"The money," I muttered, "it's buried under the third willow tree". And that's all I remembered—anesthesia services $1,536: $8.00 per minute. I never saw the recovery room—one hour: $764 plus $50 for extra 10 minutes—but when I consciously awoke, I was staring at a tiled ceiling—room charges for three days $4,716. I'll bet

**ROOM $4,716**

Michelangelo didn't even get that much for painting the Sistine Chapel's ceiling. Blank as mine was, I was to get to know that ceiling well. My immediate concern, though, was to have someone pull the ax out of my lower back—surgery @ $146 per minute = $28,032. A nurse's voice welcomed me back and handed me a button with a cord

**SURGERY $28,032**

attached. "Here," she said, "Push this. You'll feel better. It's morphine"—$116.84. Total pharmaceutical: $1,915.55.

**PHARMACY $1,915.55**

I pushed it. The nurse leaned over and whispered, "But don't push it too much; every time you push it they charge you for it." The button, I quickly discovered, was regulated, restricting me from downing the entire drip bag for permanent relief; that, or to keep me from instant financial ruin. I spent the early morning with my thumb firmly in place on the button, waiting for it to reactivate. I drifted in and out of consciousness. The ceiling tiles clarity waxed and waned. The day shift came on, and two cute young nurses' aides informed me it was time for a bed bath and pulled back my covers. Not only was it embarrassing enough to have two unknown women suddenly expose me, but I was mortified when I realized that not only was I attached to an IV and morphine drip, but my member was intimately connected to a tube to which it had not been properly introduced.

If I thought I was going to get any rest, I was mistaken. The surgeon made a cameo visit, questioned me, moved my feet about, looked at my wound then declared the operation a success. Food services wanted me to order a meal. Nurses and nurses' aides kept checking me, scanning my wrist band every time they did something to me or the machine I was attached to, a machine that was faulty because it gave false beeps, and a maintenance man kept trying to fix it, but every time it beeped the nurses came running in, thinking something was wrong. Then physical therapy—$1,092—visited, followed by occupational therapy—$234—but I may have mixed them up because anything physical I always thought of as occupational anyway. I never have known the difference. Just as I was dozing off, food services brought me a meal I couldn't eat. All I wanted was to push my button.

The next day I weaned myself off the morphine, but by then the consequences were already apparent. "Do you know what a suppository—$8.67—is?" the youngest and most attractive nurse yet asked.

"Yeah, it's that thing my grandmother always mistook as a hearing aid." Too busy being flippant I suddenly realized why she asked. "You're not going to . . . "

"Roll on your side, would you please?

"But you're not . . . "

She did.

"Now," she said, "it's time to get rid of that catheter. This doesn't hurt a bit." Which was easy for her to say.

"EeeeOwww," I bellowed.—Pain: 7. Embarrassment: 20. For the first time in my life I was glad I was not well-endowed.

After two and a half days I'd had enough. I asked to be discharged and the hospital gods consented, but not before sending a finance rep. She was vague about the bill, however, hinting that it was probably going to surpass the GNP of Lichtenstein. Her last words were, "But remember, there's no such thing as debtor's prison." As a patient, this is always comforting news—hospital total $62,280. Screws alone were $1,346 each. Wait: WHAT? You heard me, $1,346! Each! Now times that by six = $8,076. Additional hardware and glue $14,742.

**TOTAL $62,280**

What a screwing! This was beginning to sound like a Texan textbook math problem. Whit goes in for a back problem and gets 6 screws put in his spine. Each screw costs $1,346. What is the cost of the screwdriver that screws them in? Does Home Depot carry them? What if the insurance company only pays in base eight? With court costs? What would be the total then? What do you think ruined Whit's back anyway[3]? How come the other 49 states still use educational textbooks written by Republican Texan nut jobs anyway?

**SCREWING $14,742**

This begged many more questions. Like: Will the screws cause electrolysis on my

---

3. Hay bales, boulders, firewood, youth.

fillings? Why have I been losing money in the stock market all these years when a back operation increases my value by $22,818 in a matter of hours? Why can't I just replace them with construction-grade sheetrock screws and sell the titanium ones on eBay? Why aren't trust-fund punks wearing them in their faces? You know, that sort of just-fell-face-first-into-the-screw-bin look: a screw through the tongue; two screwed though the nose; several more drilled into the temples; a row of them through the eyebrows. I can't think of anything more charming. Did Frankenstein's monster have titanium screws? Do you think the monster would have liked punk rock? Richard Wagner? What's the difference between back fusion and back fission?

Over the next week I recovered bit by bit. There was no searing pain and my feet weren't numb any longer. The ax in my back—pain: 8—on the operation site began feeling like no more than a Swiss army knife stab—pain: 3. The worst part of recovering was not being able to move my bowels. I won't go into detail about what was tried; let's just say it was a four-day drought. After that, the problem was simply solved by a visiting Scottish doctor. Since I was not to pick up anything over five pounds, I let him wash the dishes. He washed them in detergent and didn't rinse them. For an entire day I didn't dare stray from the bathroom. "Hmmff." he exclaimed, "Works quicker than haggis."

"BUT REMEMBER, THERE'S NO SUCH THING AS DEBTOR'S PRISON."

Going for my follow-up—another x-ray $254—I finally saw my MRI. The physician's assistant showed a shot of my back where it looked textbook normal and even I understood it. Then she progressed down the spine into the "interesting" area. The picture became increasingly cluttered, like an amoeba-led Occupy Spine Street protest. There was a cyst and an out-of-whack disc both pushing on the spinal cord constraining its passage.

After seeing the MRI of my back, I realized how evolution, being impatient to let us stand up-right, short-changed us, giving us the wrong dynamics to do so. However, it's not all bad, as there are many who benefit from our inherent design flaw, like all the people I'm receiving get well cards from: the hospital office staff, the nurses, nurse aides, the physical therapist, the occupational therapist, the surgeon, the janitors, the maintenance man who tried to fix my machine, food services, union bosses, and state and federal inspectors. It's been very thoughtful of them, but I'm sure they will eventually want money from me—even the patient who mistakenly wandered into my room. They will probably charge me for the get well cards as well—$2.95 each—not to mention the cost of stamps—44 cents plus a stamp-application fee of 40 cents per stamp. So if you need your money in a hurry meet me at the local pawn shop where I plan on pawning my screws.

# 13

# BUMMERS

> BUMMERS DO NOT LEAD. NOT LIKE THIS QUESTION OR LIKE SHEEP TO SLAUGHTER. THEY DON'T LEAD AT ALL.

According to all the dictionaries that have apparently copied each other's websites, the word bummer, comes from the German word for loafer, bummler. Yet not one of these lexicon sites lists bummer as an orphan lamb. Then again we are dealing with minds so twisted with doubtful information they couldn't tell you if a mad cow nays or oinks. Only a Quaker website defines bummer as: A lamb rejected or forgotten by its mother and/or a lamb bumming milk from a ewe other than its mother. If we carry this thought, it seems a cloned sheep could be called a bummer also since their cells have been bummed from another sheep. But I'm not about to get into cellular clone calls. As it is, without the clones, there are already over a billion sheep on the planet and the planet doesn't need any more sheep; certainly not the two bummers that suddenly began inhabiting my world. But there they were.

"How can you refuse them?" Kim, the rancher who was trying to give them to me, asked. It was a leading question.'

Bummers do not lead. Not like this question or like sheep to slaughter: They don't lead at all.

Kim belongs to the only family in the county who run sheep in large numbers, her parents run a band and, this year Kim leased her own band. Kim's profit would be in the forthcoming lambs. Only the lambs didn't come when they were supposed to and, when they did, the weather turned foul.

I stopped by to see how it was going. It was not good.

Little hopeful orphans were everywhere staring at me with their bright, button eyes, their ears sticking out of their heads sideways like propeller blades. How could nature so recklessly consign something so innocent and adorable to such a dark fate? I knew right there, that nothing is more sorrowful than the wondering eyes of an abandoned lamb.

Two words, when coupled, should carry the Surgeon General's warning: cute and compulsion.

"All right," I said, "I'll take one."

"No, you'll take two," Kim, replied "You'll need at least two to keep each other company."

But which two? It was the bummer version of Sophie's Choice. Fortunately Kim decided for me, "Here," she said, "These two should make it."

TWO WORDS, WHEN COUPLED, SHOULD CARRY THE SURGEON GENERAL'S WARNING: CUTE AND COMPULSION. "ALL RIGHT," I SAID; "I'LL TAKE ONE." "NO, YOU'LL TAKE TWO."

I proceeded to the feed store. Talk about being fleeced. The owner raised his eyebrows. "You don't know what you're getting into, do you?" he said.

Confirming that I didn't, he handed me my bill and from the gleam in his eye I knew how a drug dealer looks when acquiring a new client. Nipples, bottles, and three bags full of milk replacer and sheep starter: $126.

I didn't even spend that much on my prom date in high school.

Driving home my bummers decided that they had had enough and, breaking out of their box, they also broke from their reputed idiom, quiet as a lamb. The noise level exceeded triple-digit decibels. The lambs weren't too meek about it either.

Or gentle as.

Or innocent as.

When I set them down on the porch, the bummers gazed at me for a few moments with curious innocence— what I'd like to believe was politeness, but then, seeing the back door open, they bolted for it. Remember the closing credits of the Flintstones? When Fred puts Dino out, but Dino runs back in, beating Fred, and locks the door on him? Well the bummers didn't slam the door on me, but they did take a running tour of the house. Now I don't know if Dino was housebroken but I can tell you, lamb poop is not sheep poop and doesn't come in carpet-friendly little balls. It comes in brown glue form and stains everything it comes in contact with.

> I DIDN'T EVEN SPEND THAT MUCH ON MY PROM DATE IN HIGH SCHOOL

It was then and there the bummers decided the house was theirs.

"See," I said to myself, "You knew this would happen."

We compromised: They stayed inside at night in the mudroom. I barricaded them in with a table laid on its side fortified with chairs. They complained loudly. They didn't like being left alone in the dark. I shut my bedroom door and tried anything but counting sheep to attempt sleep. And just when I nodded off there was a scratching at my door. I startled awake and into my own horror movie, *Night of the Hungry Bummers*. The lambs had broken out and were demanding a midnight meal.

The fastest way to a sheep's heart is through all four of its stomachs.

As they grew, despite their continued food-or-you-don't-sleep extortion plan, the lambs mostly maintained their innocence. I even felt guilty when they sniffed my sheepskin bedroom slippers. I'm sure glad I don't have to explain the facts of sheep life to them: "Well yes those are made of sheepskin but it only comes from evil sheep—Rottweiler sheep, bred by the neo-Nazis. They roam in packs and hump peoples' legs."

By the day I see the bummers grow even more. They don't have names but maybe that's part of being a bummer. I've realized what a burden it must be being a mother; what miracle lactation is. I appreciate where milk comes from, not the mix powder with warm water and put in bottles kind. It was a distant hope that they would mow the lawn and I could stop buying gas for the mower and food for them. Instead they ignore the lawn and are demolishing the flower garden. They aren't the companions I expected but then I'm not the mother they expected either. But they have bonded to me and I enjoy them more than I'm willing to show. I'm assured by my friends that my bummers are not normal pets, that I should have gotten a puppy or even compromised with a sheep dog.

The bummers have become solid packages of raw energy. They have taken to chasing cars and last week one bit the fed-ex girl. They live outside now. They are beginning to wander. They don't want to be penned up. I get anxious about them. I feel their lives suddenly heading towards the common meaning of bummer: *A situation in which no desirable result can occur.*

7 sheep years equals 1 human year.

Definitions though mean nothing to them. They live their own lives by their own time clock, with their own fates waiting. Sadly, but eventually, one day I know they will be gone. I assure them I'm not going to eat them but I try and tell them about the coyotes and the wolves and the cougars who would. They don't listen. They don't seem to care. It's just all part of being a bummer.

Bummer.

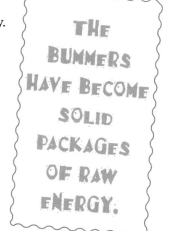

THE BUMMERS HAVE BECOME SOLID PACKAGES OF RAW ENERGY.

# THe CeNTiPeDe

How do you make your legs agree

Which way you're going to proceed?

Which legs do you make follow?

Which legs do you make lead?

Isn't it a problem, running at full speed?

Good golly Moses, centipede,

Just one of you makes a stampede!

BE PREPARED

A MIRACULOUS

So that's who you are!" I said.

"Yeah, that's who I am all right."

"I know all about you."

"What do you *really* know about me?"

"What the papers said."

"The papers don't know a damn thing!"

"You did it, though."

"You bet I did. . . . And you would have too!"

"Not me."

"You know facts but not truth."

I said nothing.

"You wanna hear?"

The cigarette I gave him glowed hard. He leaned back as the smoke seemed to melt him. He crimped his lips releasing a long string of smoke which looked more like pent-up frustration, if you know what I mean. As he spoke he no longer looked at me. He looked way off, like all newcomers here, looking, I knew, at what could have been. This was his story:

"I had it nice. Thirty thou a year. Thirty thou just for guardin' the view deck of the Davis building. 'Twenty-second highest building west of the Mississippi, ma'am,' and, 'No, ma'am, no one's jumped from here, not since I've started working here.' It was the softest job a man could have. That's all I had to do, tell gawkers how high they was and stop nuts from leapin' off. It was the nuts I owed my job to. Before me, before they had a guard, some loose-wire went up there and took the plunge, then the next thing the Davis people knew, everyone and their short-circuited brother was up there leaping off. That's bad publicity, man! Soon Davis was losing all their leasers. I don't mean to mislead you; it wasn't the leasers leapin', it was just that the leasers got tired of looking at the messes on the sidewalk. Bad for the morale. That's when I got hired.

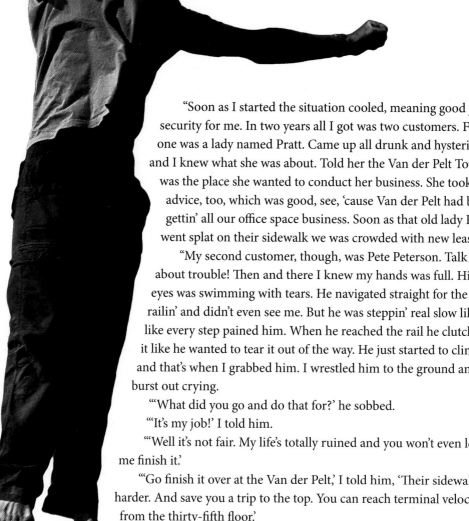

"Soon as I started the situation cooled, meaning good job
security for me. In two years all I got was two customers. First
one was a lady named Pratt. Came up all drunk and hysterical
and I knew what she was about. Told her the Van der Pelt Towers
was the place she wanted to conduct her business. She took my
advice, too, which was good, see, 'cause Van der Pelt had been
gettin' all our office space business. Soon as that old lady Pratt
went splat on their sidewalk we was crowded with new leasers.

"My second customer, though, was Pete Peterson. Talk
about trouble! Then and there I knew my hands was full. His
eyes was swimming with tears. He navigated straight for the
railin' and didn't even see me. But he was steppin' real slow like,
like every step pained him. When he reached the rail he clutched
it like he wanted to tear it out of the way. He just started to climb
and that's when I grabbed him. I wrestled him to the ground and he
burst out crying.

"'What did you go and do that for?' he sobbed.

"'It's my job!' I told him.

"'Well it's not fair. My life's totally ruined and you won't even let
me finish it.'

"'Go finish it over at the Van der Pelt,' I told him, 'Their sidewalk's
harder. And save you a trip to the top. You can reach terminal velocity
from the thirty-fifth floor.'

"'Now you're makin' fun of me,' he says, 'You know how much
guts it took me to come up here?'

"I said, 'I'm not interested. All I'm interested in is keeping your guts off our sidewalk. It's
my job to stop people like you from leapin' off this here building!'

"'Can't you let go of me?'

"'Why the hell you wanna jump anyway? You look like you still got fifty good years in
front of you.'

"'I did till yesterday.'

"'Why yesterday?'

"By this time we were both standing, but I still held his lapels.

"'You let go of me, I'll tell you.'

"So I let go. He sucked in a couple a big sobs, then talked.

"This was his story:

I had it made. Thirty-five grand a year working for Starstrums—aircraft parts. Had a cozy apartment, car paid off, money stewing in the bank, then Starstrum starts taking the slide. Pretty soon half the company was laid off, including me. Nothing bad though, there was a defense contract brewing and I heard Starstrum was lining the right pockets again and it'd just be a matter of time before I got hired back on. I figured what the hell? This is vacation time. I'll go see the world.

Well, like I said, my car was paid for. Money in the bank. That and I'd latched on to some dynamite stock. I left everything up to my mom. Nothing complicated. I let the insurance lapse on the car and left her the keys in case she had to move it. Put her name on my bank account so she could wire me money overseas. Told her when to sell the stock: May 10th. See, I guess it wasn't a real stock; I forget the word for it other than "scam." Heard about it from a friend of a friend. That sort of thing. And sell by May 10th or I'd lose my shirt. I stood to clear twenty grand.

I flew to London. Rain and fog for three weeks so I hightailed it to Greece. But let me tell you, even Greece isn't a vacation in February; rained the whole two weeks I was there. I met a girl, though, who had just come back from Kenya. Had a great time. I hadn't thought of Africa when I left the States, but with all that rain it sounded real good, and Kenya *was* good. Spent a whole month going on safaris but then the rains came there, too. Starstrum hadn't got their contract yet so I figured what the hell, might as well go right round the world.

Hit Bombay—couldn't leave it fast enough—then Delhi. Spent another day leaving that and wound up in Kathmandu. Man! I didn't know there were places like that on earth! Little temples all over and goats getting their throats cut everywhere you looked. It's a filthy place. Got sick, but everyone does there. But I liked the place. I went on some treks, even saw Everest. This was the middle of April. I was writing Mom pretty regularly, just to keep reminding her about unloading that stock, that and to wire some money to Bangkok. I gave her an address of a bank.

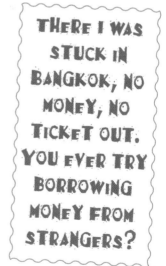

THERE I WAS STUCK IN BANGKOK, NO MONEY, NO TICKET OUT. YOU EVER TRY BORROWING MONEY FROM STRANGERS?

Well I got to Bangkok and no mail, no money. So I called home. That's when my trouble began.

Mom said, "Really, Peter, you should have got your money by now."

I said, "Standard Bank has no record of it."

"But it was too expensive. The bank was going to charge you twenty-five dollars to wire it so instead I sent it cash to general delivery. Mister Mulligan at the post office, he's so helpful, said mail to Thailand only takes five days now. Really, Peter, you should have got it!"

I hung up on her I was so pissed off. Saved me twenty-five bucks and lost me seven hundred. Forgot to even tell her about the stock. Anyway, there I was stuck in Bangkok, no money, no ticket out. You ever try borrowing money from strangers? The Embassy was no help either. I was desperate, living on credit at the hotel. Then one day this guy approaches me and says he'd take care of everything. All I had to do was carry an extra piece of baggage on the plane.

Don't ask me what it was. All I know is I sure sweated through customs; then I was met by some guy in sunglasses who took the bag—he didn't even offer me a ride home. Had to bum a quarter just to call and have Mom pick me up.

Well Mom sees me, says I'm looking well and all that, then just keeps right on talking. I didn't say a thing till we pulled in the driveway and saw the side of my car smashed in. I mean *smashed*.

"Oh that!" Mom says. "That was done at Liu Tiem's."

"But I didn't give you the keys to drive it, just move it! What's Liu Tiem's?"

"Not what, Peter. Who. Liu Tiem's the Vietnamese refugee Reverend Sandersen said we should all help out. It's really a sad story, Peter. Liu Tiem was actually a high-ranking official in the Vietnamese government. Now, in America, he can't even get a job. Reverend Sandersen said we could help out by taking our cars to Liu Tiem's and having him flush the radiators."

"You mean you had my radiator flushed?"

"Why certainly! For forty dollars, it was such a bargain!"

"*Forty dollars!*"

"Why yes. Mr. Tiem is really such a kind man. While your car was there though, Peter, Mrs. Tiem backed into it. Mr. Tiem said he would have it fixed but I started to think and thought somehow it might get Mrs. Tiem into trouble. You see she doesn't have a driver's license and really, Peter, they are such *nice* people."

"But my radiator didn't need flushing."

"Yes, but he does such nice work."

I opened the hood. The radiator had been flushed all right. Mr. Tiem had filled it back up with water which froze and now my block was cracked. I thought I was sick but I was mistaken.

I went in the house and said, "I hope my check from the stock has shown up."

"Oh that," says Mom. "I've got a little apology to make. You see as soon as you gave me that to watch I became very interested in it. I followed it daily. It did very well. It just kept going up and up. In fact it did

THE RADIATOR HAD BEEN FLUSHED. FILLED IT BACK UP WITH WATER WHICH FROZE AND NOW MY BLOCK WAS CRACKED.

so well, I took everything out of your bank account, except for what I sent you in Thailand, and I bought some more of it. Then I don't know what happened. In fact, I still don't understand. They simply stopped listing it in the paper! I even called information and got the company's number in New Jersey but all I got was a recording saying the number had been disconnected."

"*You mean you didn't sell it!*"

"Why certainly not! Not when it was doing so well! Now surely there must be some mistake."

Now I knew I was sick. I felt like crying. I said I had a bad case of jet lag and locked myself in my room. I lay there thinking how I'd lost everything—yet there was still hope. There was Starstrum. When I heard Mom go out I called up my old boss. He said, "I'm sorry but I called your mom like you told me to let you know we were hiring but she said judging by your letters you weren't going to be home for at least another six months. I had no way of contacting you. Your spot's been filled. Sorry."

"Maybe there's something else?" I asked.

He says, "Sorry, Pete. Can't help you now."

I went back to my room and I laid there all yesterday and last night and I've given it lots of thought. It's just no use. So I came here."

"By then I was seeing Pete's view twenty-twenty. I said, 'I don't blame you. I'll tell you what. I'll take my coffee break and you go ahead and jump. You just climb right over that railing there and do what you have to do.'

"Well just as his face lights up and he says, 'You sure?' the glass doors swing open and there stands an old pear-shaped woman I'd seen a thousand times up there before.

"'Peter!' she cries, 'How on earth did you know I come up here Thursdays after I help Reverend Sandersen sort used clothes? You wouldn't believe the rubbish people donate—and all the dust! That's why I come here. The fresh air. It's wonderful don't you think? Isn't the view simply marvelous?'

"It was as if I'd known Pete all his life. There was no question what had to be done. We grabbed her at once and dragged her to the railing. She grunted and panted but never managed to say anything coherent. It was like wrestling a pig in a gunnysack. We struggled and heaved and finally managed to roll her over and. . . .

"Well, *how* the *hell* were we supposed to know there was a taxi illegally parked on the sidewalk? And that her injuries wouldn't turn out worse than a coupla cuts and a broken leg? And that she was gonna kill the poor innocent cab driver? A 'Miraculous Tragedy'—that's what the papers called it. And for that I get twenty years."

"What did Pete get?" I asked.

"Don't know, time-wise. They sent him to the mental wing. Heard he's doing okay 'cept for the first Tuesday of every month. That's when his mom visits him and brings him cookies. So what are you in for?"

# Flee Fly Flow Flung

To Ben McDuff poor Mary would cling

When Ben McDuff did his highland fling

But so fast did he fing that she came unclung

And over Scottish highlands she was flung.

NICE DAY FOR

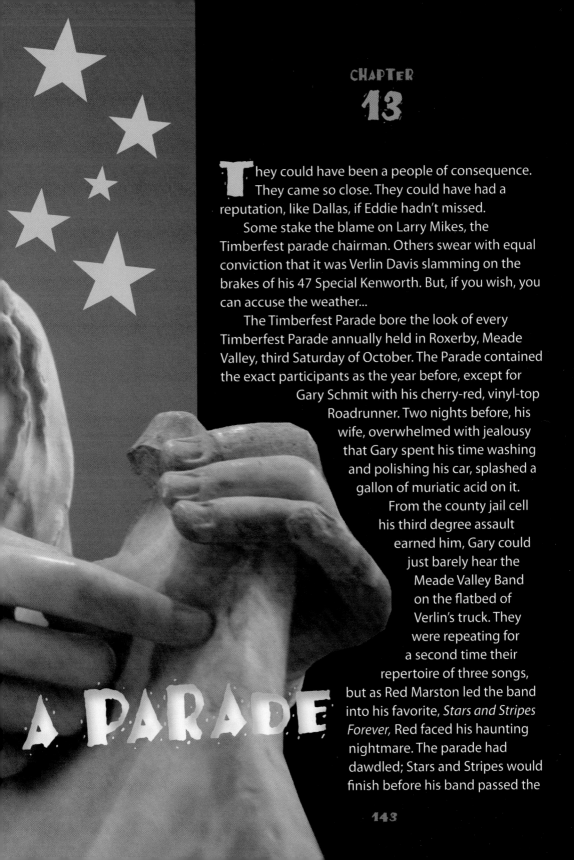

They could have been a people of consequence. They came so close. They could have had a reputation, like Dallas, if Eddie hadn't missed.

Some stake the blame on Larry Mikes, the Timberfest parade chairman. Others swear with equal conviction that it was Verlin Davis slamming on the brakes of his 47 Special Kenworth. But, if you wish, you can accuse the weather...

The Timberfest Parade bore the look of every Timberfest Parade annually held in Roxerby, Meade Valley, third Saturday of October. The Parade contained the exact participants as the year before, except for Gary Schmit with his cherry-red, vinyl-top Roadrunner. Two nights before, his wife, overwhelmed with jealousy that Gary spent his time washing and polishing his car, splashed a gallon of muriatic acid on it. From the county jail cell his third degree assault earned him, Gary could just barely hear the Meade Valley Band on the flatbed of Verlin's truck. They were repeating for a second time their repertoire of three songs, but as Red Marston led the band into his favorite, *Stars and Stripes Forever,* Red faced his haunting nightmare. The parade had dawdled; Stars and Stripes would finish before his band passed the

A PARADE

review stand. "Sheeit," Red hissed a little more audibly than he wanted as he closed the piece.

"Sheeit!" Three-and-a-half-year old Joe Billings on the sidewalk repeated and giggled. His mom belted him so hard on the ear that Joe, forever after, heard things accompanied with a remote ringing.

"Stars and Stripes," Red commanded. "Stars and Stripes, Stars and Stripes," each layer of band restated in soft tones to the tier behind. Pages were fingered back. Red raised his baton and Stars and Stripes began once more...

There was no way Red could have seen little Billy Frekkas dart out in front of Verlin's truck. Billy sought an errant mini Tootsie Roll that lay on the yellow line, the result of an arthritic Shriner's toss. Billy was only a hand's snatch away from his prize when he realized his gross misjudgment of the truck's ever-increasing presence. A faster kid could have escaped. Billy, though, hailed from a welfare crop not known for its quickness. Only the night before he had been teased to tears for his indecisiveness. In custody of his aunt, June Bledlowe, her boyfriend, Pete Haugdin, and half a dozen others who were distantly inbred, Billy and his older half-brothers, for the reward of a bowl each of chocolate ice cream, were required to name their fathers. All, except Billy, guessed according to what was commonly believed. Billy couldn't resolve

whether it was Rocky Galm or Dale Elvers. Pete laughed so hard that he fell off his chair, spraining his wrist so badly that he had to drink beer from his other hand; Dale Elvers had never been considered a candidate before.

Unlike Red, Verlin could have seen Billy's dash, but didn't. Instead, he had been infinitely eyeing the Timberfest Queen, seventeen-year-old Meg Williams, riding on the parade's lone float immediately in front of him. As Verlin perused Meg's legs, tickling his truck's brakes he heard snatches of an irritating screeching that wafted in, sandwiched between the noise of the Meade Valley Band and his engine. Brakes, he thought, mistaking the noise for what was really the First Methodist Marching Choir. Five positions ahead, the Choir too could hear the Meade Valley Band, causing them to lose both key and time. The First Methodist Marching Choir stopped once again to attempt a fresh start and Verlin's thoughts, led by his eyes, immediately returned to Meg's legs. So far it had been a breezeless morning but at that moment a mini williwaw, personalized just for Verlin, rushed over Stendal's Drug and caught both of Meg's arms raised in the middle of a tread-water wave. Her blue-frilled dress mushroomed up over her face. Verlin jolted in disbelief.

> THERE WAS NO WAY RED COULD HAVE SEEN LITTLE BILLY FREKKAS DART OUT IN FRONT OF VERLIN'S TRUCK SEEKING AN ERRANT MINI TOOTSIE ROLL.

Parrying for their assigned positions before the parade, Meg had received an avalanche of comments on her pristine appearance, mostly from the First Methodist Marching Choir. While several even touched her, they said in feigned gasps, "Oh Meg! You look simply wonderful!" along with several other platitudes of the same species. And even as she smiled and thanked them and hurried away the women continued: "Just marvelous." "Lovely." "Truly a queen." "Such a charming outfit on such a nice, deserving young lady."

Which were basically Chip Sorensen's thoughts. Chip was Meg's boyfriend and quarterback for the high school team. Chip was the son of Chas Sorensen Jr., owner of the Lily White silver mine, and the grandson of Chas Sorensen Sr., who opened the mine (naming it after his wife). Chas Sr. settled up with his Chinese labor by sending them over what is now called Chinaman Falls on a log raft. With five minutes before the parade's start, Chip shepherded Meg into the old Antlers Hotel-cum-cheap-rent-apartments and under the stairwell impregnated her in 29 seconds (completely unaware that he had been conceived just 200 feet away in the alley between Main and Washington in only 13 seconds). Unfortunately, things removed for the act were not carefully inventoried; thus, they were not put back. One of these was Meg's lipstick;

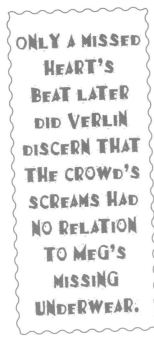

ONLY A MISSED HEART'S BEAT LATER DID VERLIN DISCERN THAT THE CROWD'S SCREAMS HAD NO RELATION TO MEG'S MISSING UNDERWEAR.

another was her panties, which, during the strategic shuffle for positioning of feet got shoved into a substance which, when Meg's eyes focused in the half-tone darkness, was thought to be a wino's vomit.

Only a missed heart's beat later did Verlin discern that the crowd's screams had no relation to Meg's missing underwear. Later, he thought he could even remember the crowd's communal look of horror as a child disappeared under his truck as he slammed on the brakes. Over more screams there was the discordant explosion of instruments receiving unexpected blasts of air, the clatter of brass on pavement, followed by the groans of the instrument's owners who lay scattered amongst the wreckage.

Ten positions ahead of Verlin, Lyle Love was the lone Shriner who caught a glimpse of the Meade Valley Band spilling onto the pavement. Lyle had just seen his granddaughter in the crowd and was circling back in his motorized bathtub with an extra-large handful of Tootsie Rolls for her when he witnessed the disaster. In one fluid move his hand went from its toss to the gearshift. In second gear he skirted the flock of Meade Valley cheerleaders, nearly sideswiped the St. Marie's Ambulance and caused Mib Johnson's horse to rear; in third he scattered the First Methodist Marching Choir—but that is all the farther he got.

The Knights of Columbus, still unaware of what Verlin had just done to the Meade Valley Band, had been watching Lyle's errant behavior the whole way towards them. He was about to receive three-years' accumulation of their wrath plus interest, because for three years Larry Mikes had positioned the Knights behind the Shriners. Larry, himself was not a Shriner, but his sister was married to Lyle Love.

Although it was Frank Higgens who screeched, "Hold the line boys!" each Knight later claimed credit to the battle cry. Lyle swerved but his bathtub did not adhere to high-speed performance. With his overturned tub skidding close behind him, Lyle plowed into the wall of Knights...

Which was exactly the moment Jack Sibber alerted the other Shriners. They saw Lyle disappear under a pile of Knights. The four remaining bathtubs vanguarded the attack; the other ten Shriners, anger suppressing their handicap of fat and arthritis, leapt from their Cadillac convertible and followed at what they thought was both a run and a heroic speed.

As the formation of bathtubs raced back down the street, the cheerleaders burst into tears and Mib Johnson was at last bucked off his horse. The bathtub Shriners

believed the velocity and bulk of their tubs would earn them a quick victory but they were wrong. Three tubs were quickly boarded by Knights and overturned.

Only John Ellingstrom remained in action. In a slower tub he had watched the ill-fated charge. Then he spotted Dick Miller who was just getting to his feet after being knocked down. John tried mowing him down but Dick neatly sidestepped the attack.

Instead, it was Mary McCarthy who finished off John. Mary held no allegiance with the Knights. She just knew an opportunity when she saw one. Her husband, Andy, had worked in John Ellingstrom's mill for twenty-five years when one day, cleaning out the hog, someone switched it back on. There was more of Andy that was hosed down the drain than got buried. The accident had happened ten days before the annual Ellingstrom Christmas banquet; now, ten months later Mary still burned at not being invited. John received the full weight of Mary's Mary Kay cosmetic-filled purse in his face, knocking him cold and sending him broadside into Mac Sill's pickup that carried the Meade Valley Little League Baseball team, Lower Northwest Regional Champions.

Even before the wayward squall blew Meg's skirt up and the subsequent chaos ensued, the team was acting up. With an overabundance of hormones, boredom and orneriness they already were winging candy at the spectators. Stalled, with disaster fore and aft, they eagerly entered the ruckus and began pelting the clients of St. Marie's Nursing Home, Meade Valley's low-cost quarters not only for the elderly but also for, as the valley referred to them, the "mentally maimed." Darryl Squires, the pitcher, wound up and was just unleashing a Bach's butterscotch at a hydrocephalic when John smashed into the truck. The throw instead hit Eddie Tammes in the right eye.

Fortunately, all of Meade Valley's emergency vehicles were participating in the parade, and if there was a positive view to be taken about the disaster it was as if the parade had been tailored for their services. It took the combined efforts of the State Police, Sheriff and City Police to squelch the Shriner-Knight riot and the St. Marie's ambulance, Meade Valley Aid car and Fire Department to handle the injuries which were so numerous that it would be impossible to list exactly what happened to whom. There were twenty-eight broken bones ranging from a pelvis to a little finger; two punctured lungs; no official tally of sprains and abrasions; and forty-six teeth were lost or removed, not counting Peter Miller who had to have his dentures surgically removed from his throat after being knocked there by his tuba mouthpiece. Larry Mikes suffered a heart attack from which he never recovered.

As for Billy Frekkas, he was merely knocked down by Verlin's truck but not run over. The impact of his head bouncing on pavement did not (using his four older half-brothers to measure against) seem to exacerbate his slowness.

The lone injury of consequence was that to Eddie Tammes. Eddie was seventeen and his sole love was for guns. Only the year before, the FBI nailed him for selling a fully automatic Uzi, which he had bought from an Israeli exchange student, to an Aryan race member. The Bach's butterscotch had merely bruised Eddie's eye but Eddie was the lone child of a Valium-addicted mother who doted over him and insisted on taking him to Doctor Milligan, Meade Valley's alcoholic optometrist.

Doc Milligan had not attended the parade; he was too hung-over. His phone had rung over twenty times before he disconnected it. It was Lyla Thorton, his nurse, and Rose Tammes (who had all but held Lyla hostage) who spurred him out of bed.

"My Eddie's been blinded," said Rose trying to hold back tears and the temptation to pop two more Valiums.

Without even glancing at Eddie, Doctor Milligan told Lyla to take Eddie to his office, which helped comfort his wretchedness for he knew what he could charge for an emergency operation. Anything to help smooth the cost of his messy divorce.

The two whiskey sours he chased these thoughts with also helped his outlook, though it didn't stop his hands trembling. Of course the only thing Doc Milligan could have done to save the eye was not to operate. Lyla knew this, too. She also knew he would blow the operation, but being the highest paid nurse in the valley and with an extreme dislike for Rose Tammes, she said nothing.

AS FOR BILLY FREKKAS, HE WAS MERELY KNOCKED DOWN BUT NOT RUN OVER.

From the day of the surgery onward, Eddie could only discern splotches of light from his right eye. Upon learning this, Rose Tammes swore and cried and swallowed handfuls of Valiums and said Eddie now would never amount to anything—and she was right. He never did learn to properly aim a gun with his left eye, which caused his one shot to go wild—the one he fired at the 43rd President of the United States.

## MODEL Y

Henry Ford went to town

Feeling autographic.

Wrote his name upon a car

And called it auto traffic.

Charles Darwin fled from town

Feeling less than regal

Summed up his notes concluding that

He'd descended from a Beagle.

## PET PORCUPINES

Pet porcupines require love

But always pet them with a glove.

# THE HIPPOPOTOMOUSE

A rare and dangerous species

Is the hippopotomouse.

If you get one in your attic

Then you'd better leave your house.

# THE RATTLESNAKE

The rattle is maybe

Because he's part baby

But check his diaper

You'll see he's a viper.